Outside
the Wire

Outside the Wire

TEN LESSONS I'VE LEARNED
IN EVERYDAY COURAGE

Jason Kander

TWELVE

NEW YORK   BOSTON

Twelve
Hachette Book Group
1290 Avenue of the Americas, New York, NY 10104
twelvebooks.com
twitter.com/twelvebooks

First edition: August 2018

Twelve is an imprint of Grand Central Publishing. The Twelve name
and logo are trademarks of Hachette Book Group, Inc.

The publisher is not responsible for websites (or their content) that are
not owned by the publisher.

The Hachette Speakers Bureau provides a wide range of authors
for speaking events. To find out more, go to
www.hachettespeakersbureau.com or call (866) 376-6591.

Library of Congress Control Number: 2018940084

ISBNs: 978-1-5387-4759-9 (hardcover); 978-1-5387-4761-2 (ebook)

Printed in the United States of America

LSC-C

10 9 8 7 6 5 4 3 2 1

To Diana. My teammate, my soul mate, and my best friend. (ILYM!)

Contents

Contents

Introduction

When you get ready to deploy, you go through a bunch of training. I did my convoy training during intelligence school with Humvees that weren't armored, but we were told, you'll have the real deal when you get *over there*. The idea that it would be different "over there" or "downrange" was a pretty common refrain from the trainers at Fort Huachuca, Arizona. So when I got to Afghanistan and was preparing for my first convoy to the camp where I would be stationed, I was picturing the vehicles you see in the movies and on TV. Big, armored trucks or Humvees under a machine gun manned by a badass-looking infantryman the size of a house.

After all the training and all the anticipation of being in a combat zone, I was feeling pretty tough in my "battle rattle"—body armor, Kevlar helmet, pistol on my hip. *This is it*, I thought, *I'm finally going outside the wire.* I didn't even have a rifle yet, but I felt like GI Joe.

A marine captain introduced himself as the convoy commander and went over what we were to do if we were attacked and who was in charge if he was killed during the roughly one-hour trip from Bagram Air Base to Camp Eggers in Kabul. His rifle was hanging across his chest from a fancy sling and his load-bearing vest was packed with extra magazines of ammunition.

But while he was talking, I realized he was referring to the vehicles behind him, which were not at all what I had expected. "Over there" had become "over here," but these were not armored Humvees with a big machine gun on top. In fact, they weren't Humvees at all. Not even close.

I realized we were about to traverse the sometimes IED-ridden open roads of Afghanistan in unarmored Mitsubishi Pajeros.* I instantly felt a whole lot less tough. In fact, "tough" was now several country miles away from where I stood emotionally. This was, for the first time in my life, the raw physical fear of being killed.

I was sweating, my heart was pounding, and my feet felt heavy as I climbed into the Pajero's gray cloth backseat. As the new guy, I was scrunched into the middle.

I was trying to play it cool and decided I could best pull it off by not speaking or making eye contact with anyone. The navy lieutenant next to me told me to take off my Kevlar helmet. I noticed I was the only one wearing it, so I took it off, but I apparently looked confused enough

---

* An IED is an improvised explosive device, and a Mitsubishi Pajero is a midsize civilian sport utility vehicle—basically the Japanese equivalent of a Ford Escape.

that another sailor—our driver—offered me an explanation about what happens when the bad guys can make out the helmet in a far-off silhouette.

"There's no armor at all on this vehicle, so if we get blown up, we're all going to die anyway." She drew a pistol from her thigh holster, pulled back the slide, and put a round into the chamber. "If some Taliban asshole has his finger on an IED trigger, just waiting for us, it's better if it takes an extra beat for him to spot a clown car of Americans." She slid the pistol into a holster on the chest of her body armor before turning the ignition key and starting the little SUV.

The lieutenant next to me did the same with her pistol. "Basically, if you wear that thing," she said, picking up where our driver had left off, "he can see a 'bobblehead' silhouette from a lot farther away, and we go boom."

Another navy lieutenant—a guy in his late thirties—turned around to face me from the front passenger seat. "There's no armor underneath us either, so some guys prefer to sit on their Kevlar. You know, just in case you survive and wanna have kids." He turned back toward the front. "Up to you, dude."

I noticed navy guy wasn't sitting on his Kevlar, so I thought it best to go with the flow and just placed mine at my feet. Each of them had introduced themselves a few minutes prior, but my brain was too scattered to memorize any of the names yet.

I was too busy thinking, *What the hell am I doing here?*

I thought about how crazy everyone back home thought I was and, for the first time, wondered if they were right. I had left behind a well-paying job as a lawyer that included a very safe office with a nice view of the Kansas City skyline. Bagels and doughnuts were free in the conference room on Friday mornings. My wife, Diana, was probably asleep right now in our bed in our ranch house in KC's quaint and historic Waldo neighborhood.

As we slowly crept along the dirt roads of Bagram Air Base toward the front gates, my fellow carpoolers were chatting it up like it was any other road trip.

"So where ya from?"

"How was your flight?"

"How'd you like the landing?"

"The colonel's excited to have a fellow army guy inbound."

"Ha! Yeah, he's been surrounded by all us other branches lately."

I hoped I was doing a passable job of pretending I was not the most afraid I'd ever been in my life.

When we passed through the front gates, our driver put her foot down and out we went into the wild beige yonder of a distinctly unfriendly-looking dust bowl of one- and two-story buildings. It was quiet for a couple of minutes as each occupant of the car eyeballed every passing pedestrian and motorist, performing multiple individual assessments per second.

Soon the buildings became farther apart and then tapered off completely, and all I could see in any direction was a sparsely inhabited desert landscape with mountains visible on the horizons to our left and right.

Like the moon with mountains, I thought to myself.

I asked what the potential IED plan was, meaning what we were supposed to do if we saw something that could be a possible bomb buried in the road. Everyone just laughed morbidly and then told me the roads in Afghanistan were so messed up that, unlike in training, we just had to speed up and drive past, hoping for the best. If we stopped to check out everything that looked suspicious, the trip would take forever, and we'd never get to Kabul.

I remember feeling pretty nauseous right about then, and as we bumped along for close to an hour, my mouth gradually became as dry as the landscape.

We entered Kabul through a big dusty traffic circle I recognized from pictures. The male navy lieutenant in the front seat casually mentioned that there had been "a whole bunch of suicide bombings" there in the last couple of weeks.

As we wove aggressively through Kabul's crowded traffic, my physical fear had now been joined by a social fear, because I was becoming concerned about the very real possibility I might throw up on all my new coworkers.

Fortunately, we arrived safely and my breakfast stayed in my stomach.

In retrospect, the first of my many times outside the wire was entirely unremarkable. Yet it was still a formative experience in my life, because if you've been outside the wire—even once—your perspective is forever changed.

But let's return to the question I'd asked myself just before rolling out the front gates: *What the hell am I doing here?*

Like a lot of veterans my age, my life is easily divided into two parts: before and after 9/11.

Life before 9/11 was pretty simple. My parents instilled in me a deep-rooted sense of duty and obligation through the power of their example. Mom and Dad first met while working together as juvenile probation officers in Kansas City, Kansas, where my dad also worked nights as a cop. I was four when they adopted Jeff, my younger brother; and years later they began taking in neighborhood boys whose families were struggling.

They never sat Jeff and me down at the kitchen table to have a "family meeting" about these decisions; they just made up another bed and added a place setting at the dinner table. So I grew up with a strong crew of what we referred to as "unofficial foster brothers" close to my own age, all of whom remain my friends.

We lived on the semirural western edge of Shawnee, Kansas, a suburb of Kansas City, Missouri, which was the big city my family had called home for four generations.

There's nothing I would change about the way I grew up. Like anyone else, I experienced the regular childhood and teenage stress of figuring out where I fit in, tried my best to understand girls, and learned how much trouble

I could get into* with a delicate cocktail of sarcasm and charm.

My best friends came home from school with me every night, and they were there in the morning when I woke up. Life was like a slumber party interrupted only by school and sports. My dad, who for most of my childhood owned and operated a private security company, even coached our baseball team. Baseball was at the center of everything, from my friend group to my daydreams.

I was already five foot ten by eighth grade, so I didn't realize everyone else was about to catch up to me on the field. Two years and only one inch later, I realized I was a lot better at arguing than I was at baseball, so I focused on debate during the school year and made my summers all about baseball—knowing my "career" on the diamond wouldn't extend into my college years.

By the fall of 2001, I was twenty years old and thought I had a pretty solid plan for the next few years of my life. I was in my final year of college at American University in Washington, DC, and my girlfriend, Diana, was in her senior year, too, but she was back home at the University of Missouri–Kansas City. We'd been a couple since our first date in high school—my senior prom—but we'd also been apart for all of college, and being together was at the top of our list.

I was excited about going to law school, marrying Diana, moving home to Kansas City, and practicing law. I figured

---

* And out of.

I might eventually run for office, but I didn't really know what that meant yet. Joining the military was something I talked about a fair amount, but it was in the "someday" category of my life.

I had always looked up to people, including my parents, who had served. I loved seeing my dad's police uniform and badge, and, as a kid, I would stand in front of the mirror practicing my salute while wearing a uniform shirt from his security company. My great-grandfather and grandfather had served in World War I and World War II, respectively. Neither had a military "career" per se, but when war broke out they were of age, so they signed up, went off to war, did their duty, and then went back to their lives.

That simple, practical act of patriotism just made a lot of sense to me, the idea that you don't have to already be a soldier to serve your country when it goes to war. Despite my admiration for those who had served, I'm not sure whether I was on a path to ever actually do it.

As a college student, I was insecure about the fact that I'd done nothing to prove myself. I knew the toughest foes I'd ever faced down were high school pitchers and college debaters. In e-mails home to Diana, I'd express self-doubt, posing questions such as "Is a man really a man if he's never been tested?"

—————

On the morning of Tuesday, September 11, 2001, I was in DC walking across American's campus headed for a chemistry class when I overheard someone say a second plane had hit the towers. I stepped inside the student center, found a television, and watched as the anchor broke the news of a plane crashing into the Pentagon.

I was overcome with a single thought that rang in my head like a refrain: *I have to do something.*

The phone lines were down, so I headed to my apartment to fire off a few quick e-mails to reassure Diana and my family that I was safe.

My roommates and I climbed into my pickup truck and drove down near the Capitol because we had heard that they needed people to give blood. The streets were empty, and for a kid who grew up in Shawnee and thought DC was the busiest city in the world, it was completely surreal.

We found our destination and realized one of the reasons the streets were clear was that a lot of people had the same idea as we did. I don't know how long we stood in that blood-donation line, but it felt like a couple of hours at least. After all that time speculating among ourselves about what was happening—this was before everyone had Twitter in the palm of their hands—a nurse came out and told us they couldn't take any more blood.

"Thanks for waiting for so long," she said. "I hope you can find some other way to help."

My burning sense of obligation to "do something" grew even greater. I decided right then and there that I would join the military. I had no idea what that meant yet, but I was determined to see it through.

When I got back to my apartment, each of my family members had replied to my e-mails. Just like the e-mails a lot of Americans exchanged that day, they were mostly just letting me know they loved me. One of my "foster" brothers, Justin, who now lived in Denver, ended his e-mail, "I'm sure you're going to join the military, but PLEASE DO NOT JOIN TODAY!!!"

That night, when the phones started working again, I told Diana that we had been turned away at the blood bank and I had decided to join the military. Her response was immanently practical: "Can't you just go back and see if they can take blood tomorrow?"

———

The next morning, I went running for the first time in years. I timed my run to see where it stacked up against the military fitness standards, and so began a five-year sprint that had led me all the way into the front gates of Camp Eggers in Kabul.

Over the coming months, I would spend time outside the wire about four days a week, sometimes on convoys to Bagram Air Base and back. After a while, I even graduated to the occasional role of convoy commander.

The convoys came to feel pretty normal to me. It was still scary, but not "What am I doing here?" scary. Just extra-alert, slightly-elevated-adrenaline scary. Sometimes it felt so routine that I'd have to make conversation with the driver just to avoid nodding off.

One such convoy to Bagram near the end of my tour stands out. It was basically the same trip I had taken to Camp Eggers a few months before. Just like with my first convoy, I was standing there in my battle rattle, pistol on my hip, but a lot had changed.

Unlike before, I had a rifle slung over my shoulder, a few months of dust on my boots, and I was now the convoy commander. I stood in front of a small gaggle of soldiers, all of whom had either just arrived or just returned to Afghanistan from midtour leave. Same little unarmored Mitsubishi Pajeros awaiting us, but this time I had my back to them, because I was facing the group that was about to ride down to Camp Eggers.

I explained what to do if we were attacked or if there was an IED, and I let it be known who would be in charge if I got killed. I asked for a show of hands to identify the certified combat lifesavers and made sure to divide them equally into separate vehicles. I was wrapping up the convoy brief when I saw a kid who didn't look like he needed to shave more than twice a week staring back at me on what was obviously—judging by the tension on his face— his first or second day in Afghanistan. His uniform looked brand-new, and he was wearing his Kevlar helmet and even had the shoulder plates on his body armor. His eyes were wide and his face was turning a light shade of green.

I was thinking, *So that's what I looked like on my first day? Damn.*

I locked and loaded my rifle, pulled my pistol from my

hip holster, chambered a round, and slid it into the holster on my vest so that I could reach it while seated if necessary, and climbed into the front passenger seat of the lead vehicle.

I watched the green-faced kid to see what he'd do—whether he'd get in the SUV. He was looking down at the ground with his hands on his hips. He had likely figured out that nobody would say anything if he just let himself get sick and got on the schedule for some other convoy. He could put it off and hope for armored vehicles or even ask around about a helicopter ride to Kabul.

He lifted his head, took a deep breath, slugged down some water, and climbed into the SUV in a seat right behind me.

As we rolled through the front gate for his first trip outside the wire, all I could think was, *Man, I hope this kid doesn't puke on me.*

I think about that kid a lot. I think about his path to that moment, how he volunteered to sign up after 9/11, knowing he'd probably end up in a place like Afghanistan, in that seat behind me on his way outside the wire. And in that moment, he chose to put the job first and get in the Pajero.

A few minutes earlier—as he stood there composing himself—he knew the right thing to do and he knew the easy thing to do. That kid chose to do the right thing, even though it wasn't easy.

I never got his name and I never saw him again after that day, but as a politician, every time I face a hard choice on a tough or unpopular issue, I imagine trying to convince that kid what I'm doing now is scary or difficult. I've never been able to picture him buying that argument.

I think of him as exactly what we need more of in American politics—people who are willing to get in the SUV because they know it's more important than it is scary.

I think all the time about so many of the people I served with in the army, and I don't mean "They're in my thoughts," or some other trite throwaway line politicians use about veterans. I mean I think about them as if they're still next to me, judging my decisions, sizing up my moral courage.

Politicians are inundated with feedback that encourages self-importance and rewards self-preservation, so it helps to keep my fellow service members in the front of my mind as people who made more important decisions by lunch than most politicians, including me, make in a week. I'm frustrated knowing this cautious, selfish, face-saving approach to politics has become the norm, because that perception keeps good people away.

With what's going on in America right now, it's easy to look at the issues you care about, see an impossibly uphill battle, and lose the will to fight. But you picked up this book because you have at least a passing interest in changing the world. Whether it's running for office, working on a campaign, or leaving your fancy job to join a nonprofit, there's something you've always hoped you might do someday. I hope after reading this book you decide to make that someday today, because the world needs you.

We have enough people in public life who never go outside the wire. They fortify their districts with gerrymandered lines and camouflage their beliefs behind meaningless platitudes, and therefore, they'll never advance any cause beyond their own careers.

You don't have to accept the petty smallness of modern American politics in order to succeed. In life, and in politics, the most important work is often that which happens outside the wire. If you're always safe in your career, you're not doing much to help anyone other than yourself.

Between my time in uniform and my time in elected office, I've learned—often the hard way—valuable lessons about everyday courage. This book, among other things, lays out what Taco Bell taught me about enjoying life, what an Adam Sandler movie taught me about admitting mistakes, and what a heckler in a crowd taught me about humility. In dozens of bite-size military and political stories of failure, embarrassment, and success, you're going to learn what I've learned. It might save you some time.*

———

A year and a half after I came home from Afghanistan, I was elected to the Missouri House of Representatives. In my first term, I set out to reform the campaign finance and ethics laws of the state. I was a freshman member of the minority party and one of the only members who refused

———

* And some humiliation.

personal gifts from lobbyists in a state with virtually no ethics or campaign laws. My zeal for cleaning up Jefferson City was not exactly welcomed by the political establishment in either party.

I lost count of how many times a fellow legislator told me they agreed with me and appreciated what I was doing, but they just couldn't afford to help me. They were afraid of risking their chairmanship or their committee assignment or, in some cases, their office space or their parking spot. If I walked by while the Speaker of the House was talking to someone in the hallway, he'd interrupt himself to point me out, using his adorable nickname for me: "That piece of shit right there."

In hopes of intimidating me into backing off my push for reform, the leadership would refuse to recognize me to speak on the floor, kill my bills as soon as I'd file them, and once they even submitted a phony ethics complaint against me. Maybe it was easier for me to champion this issue because I was so new to politics—I didn't have a long career to lose. Maybe I just wasn't willing to surrender on one of the first big issues I tackled. Or maybe it was just that I was thinking of that green-faced kid who got in the SUV, but I stuck with it.

In 2016, Missourians passed a constitutional amendment that included quite a few of the reforms I introduced way back in 2010, and there's another initiative headed for the 2018 ballot.

So no, I did not choose the title *Outside the Wire* because

I think I'm some sort of badass war hero. In fact, I'm very far from it, and I know that a lot of people have done much more than I ever did. I've spent a lot more time figuratively outside the wire in politics than I literally did in the military, but I'd be a very different politician if I had not first been a soldier. Anyone would be.

If you picked up this book hoping for a bunch of war stories, then you'll be disappointed. I knew a ton of people in the army who did more than me, and my greatest fear in writing this book was that I would somehow disrespect them in the process of puffing myself up.

I had one four-month deployment, during which I never had to kill anyone; and I came home unharmed, so my gratitude is informed by survivor's guilt. That's why I believe the state of our democracy and the triviality of our politics is the ultimate slap in the face to the scores of veterans who gave so much more of themselves than I did.

Yes, I am fed up with politicians for whom the whole point of politics is to stay in politics, but I'm also excited by a new generation of American leaders who have voluntarily been through something in their lives more difficult than a reelection campaign.

If you're thinking of getting involved in politics or public service to do something rather than be something, then you're every bit as valuable to this nation as that kid who had the courage to get in the Pajero.

When it comes to serving others, nothing productive

happens inside the wire. If your objective is simply political or social survival, you can probably stick around a long time, but to what end?

If you want to be a part of changing the world, well, you'll eventually have to roll through the front gate.

Outside
the Wire

Courage is the most important of all the virtues, because without courage you can't practice any other virtue consistently. You can practice any virtue erratically, but nothing consistently without courage.

—Maya Angelou

Experience is good, but perspective is golden.

"Everyday courage" isn't running into a burning building, launching into space, or jumping out of a plane. Everyday courage is conquering little fears in your everyday life. Maybe it's admitting a mistake, asking for help, or refusing to let an awkward moment stop you from speaking up for a colleague whom your boss treats unfairly.

When most Americans do exhibit this kind of courage at work, they receive no accolades, because showing everyday courage is simply a synonym for being a decent person.

However, when politicians demonstrate the equivalent of everyday courage, pundits call it "political courage," which seems to mean, "doing the right thing despite being a politician."

From my perspective, we've set the bar pretty low, because I've met a politician who had to have *real* courage just to get up and go to work every day.

Whenever someone invokes the term "political courage," I think about the time I was part of a small security element escorting a new member of the Afghan Parliament home to Nangahar Province from the capital in Kabul. This was an Afghan politician living in constant danger, but not as a result of radical statements or even an agenda hostile to a particular interest group.

Instead, this elected official lived under the persistent threat of death simply because she was a woman.

Years later, as a member of the Missouri House of Representatives, I would struggle along with my colleagues with decisions none of us would remember in a year, and I would think about her.

I considered how unlikely it was she ever cared about how something polled or worried about what some lobbyist or donor might want her to do. With all she was risking just to be there and do the job, I imagined she simply did what she thought was right.

In light of the level of actual, literal courage this woman exhibited in politics, the least a politician like me can do is try to maintain some perspective over how easy it is to practice garden-variety, everyday courage.

Real tough guys don't need to prove anything.

When I first entered ROTC in 2002, the vast majority of the army had still never deployed, so the rest of us revered anyone with a combat patch. I encountered Master Sergeant Matt Eversmann during one of my very first field training exercises in ROTC. You may not know the name, but to the cadets of the Hoya Batallion, he may as well have been George Washington and Dwayne "The Rock" Johnson all rolled into one very tall human.

Not only did he walk, talk, and spit tobacco like a total stud, but he looked to be about a foot taller than Josh Hartnett, the actor who famously portrayed him in the lead role of *Black Hawk Down*, the movie about the 1993 Battle of Mogadishu.

There's zero chance he's currently aware the two of us ever met, but he made quite an impression on me during the one field training exercise he participated in with my unit.

Standing in the deep woods of Fort Belvoir, I was supposed to be tracking down a "point,"* but it was my first try at nighttime land navigation and I was hosing it up good. For a few hours, I'd been trying to save myself some embarrassment by locating at least one of the orange markers at the grid coordinates I'd been assigned, but now that my map had fully disintegrated in the pouring rain, I had lost all hope.

I took out my compass and started double-timing in the direction of the "panic azimuth" we'd been given to help lost little "cadidiots" like me make it back to the rest of the unit before the sun came up. Though I was pretty new to

---

* Small hidden signs labeled with alphanumeric codes and placed throughout the woods.

ROTC, I'd seen enough in my short time to fully expect I was about to turn in my scorecard in exchange for a dressing-down by a young, in-your-face sergeant who would let me know how many people could die if I got lost like that in combat. I also knew this would be done at a volume sure to let everyone in the vicinity know I'd failed miserably.

At this point, I could deal with the embarrassment as long as I was a few minutes closer to changing into dry underwear.

After a soggy wait in line to turn in my blank, laminated scorecard, I looked up with horror. Way up.* This wasn't going to be an ordinary kind of humiliation, because none other than Master Sergeant Eversmann himself was looking down at me from inside the warm, lit tent.

I graduated from embarrassed to mortified.

"How'd you do, Cadet?"

On the outside, I kept my eyes forward and my shoulders back, but on the inside I curled up into a ball and braced for the worst. "Not well, Sergeant. Zero points."

The biggest badass I'd ever met in real life smiled, pointed to the rifle slung over my shoulder, and asked, "You still got your weapon, right?"

"Uh, yes, Sergeant."

"Success!" he announced, raising his arms in the air like he was celebrating a touchdown.

---

* In retrospect, he's only about four inches taller than me, but I was scared, OK?

I didn't know whether I was being mocked or encouraged, so I just stood there like a dork.

"C'mon," he said, patting me on the back and waving me into the tent. "It's freezing out there, son, and we have hot coffee in here."

He knew I didn't need to be told how important it was to do better next time, so he decided to teach me a different lesson: Real tough guys don't need to prove it all the time.

When an officer came into the tent and demanded to know who had given coffee to a bunch of cadets, Master Sergeant Eversmann pointed to himself and said, "Sir, you don't have to teach soldiers how to be miserable, because they already know."

From the perspective of a career enlisted man who'd seen what he'd seen, what sense did it make to torture a bunch of waterlogged cadets for no good reason?

Some traditions are dumb and need to die.

In the Missouri House of Representatives* there used to be a tradition that you spoke only to the reporters from media

---

* Like *Slaughterhouse-Five*, this book is unstuck in time, meaning it's just pieces of my life offered up without any regard to chronological order, so to help us stay oriented, here's a basic timeline: I was born (1981); the Kansas City Royals won the World Series (1985); I met Diana and graduated high school (1999); graduated college, entered law school, and enrolled in ROTC (2002); married Diana and enlisted in the Army

outlets in your district. If someone contacted you from the little weekly paper in somebody else's district, you'd check in with your colleague from that area before granting an interview. This seemed to hold whether the person was in your party or not.

Most of these weekly papers had nobody at the capitol, so they based a lot of their reporting on information from their own elected representatives' press releases. This setup meant rural representatives sometimes enjoyed total control over how they and their party's legislative leadership were viewed back home.

Given my newbie perspective, I started accepting interviews from other legislators' hometown papers without their permission. The first couple of times, it ruffled feathers, but the result was a balanced local story. Fully emboldened, I started going even further by personally calling my colleagues' local papers and pitching stories.

For instance, I read with amazement the representative from Warrensburg's press release claiming he had cut

---

National Guard (2003); got my commission as an Army Reserve intelligence officer, graduated law school, passed the bar, and entered intelligence training (2005); voluntarily deployed to Afghanistan (2006); came home and transferred back to the Army National Guard as a combat leadership instructor (2007); was elected (2008) and reelected to the state house (2010); was honorably discharged from the Army National Guard (2011); was elected secretary of state (2012); became a dad (2013); the Royals won the World Series again (2015); ran and lost a race for the US Senate (2016); founded Let America Vote (2017); and then wrote this book (2018).

"state-funded lobbyists" in order to put money into Meals on Wheels. In reality, he'd voted to cut Meals on Wheels, and the "state-funded lobbyists" he was trying to eliminate were actually legislative liaisons in departments like health, conservation, and agriculture. These liaisons existed to help legislators assist constituents with whatever they needed, and all of us regularly took credit for their work. Many of these liaisons—before their current positions—happened to have been part of the Democratic governor's campaign staff, and this Republican state representative from Warrensburg felt that was reason enough to go after them and eliminate their jobs. So what if it screwed his constituents? I guess he was busy settling scores.

I called up the Warrensburg *Daily Star-Journal* and gave a reporter the real story about Meals on Wheels and legislative liaisons. When that story ran in the paper, my fellow legislators reacted as though I'd driven to Warrensburg's town square and vandalized *Old Drum*.* A gaggle of house members cornered me on the floor and lectured me about what an "ungentlemanly" thing I had done.

"Ungentlemanly? Lying to your constituents is pretty ungentlemanly," I said, before telling them they "could expect more where this came from." It got so heated that people in the gallery thought we might be about to throw some punches.

Nobody punched anybody, but I did just what I'd

---

* A very important statue of a very important dog.

threatened to do, and, to my knowledge, that quaint little hometown paper rule no longer exists.

Armed with a legislative rookie's point of view, I was able to look at the way things had always been done and ask, "But why?"

When nobody came up with a good answer, it didn't take much courage to end a dumb tradition.

The only scary meetings are the ones with people who can kill more than your career.

Abdul Jabar Sabet was my favorite contact within the Afghan government because he spoke fluent English, was highly placed, and had no discernible incentive to help anyone kidnap me. By the time we met in 2006, Sabet was the attorney general of Afghanistan and was engaged in a fierce campaign against corruption. As far as I could tell at the time, he was mostly legit. I say mostly because I didn't meet any Afghan government officials I knew for sure to be 100 percent legit. I had been reading intelligence reports about Sabet's anticorruption campaign back in Tampa when I'd been assigned to the US Central Command's intelligence division before deploying to Afghanistan, so I was almost starstruck when I first met him.

Others in US intelligence warned me not to place too much trust or faith in Sabet given his close ties to Gulbuddin

Hekmatyar, the leader of a dangerous terrorist network known as Hezb-e-Islami Gulbuddin (HIG).

Genuinely wanting to believe in Sabet, I thought his ties to Hekmatyar went back more to their time of working together when Hekmatyar was prime minister of Afghanistan and leader of the HIG political party—long before Hekmatyar and the HIG became a terrorist network and swore allegiance to al-Qaeda.

It was a bit of a coup when I developed such a useful relationship with the Afghan attorney general. No one could really figure out how a very green junior officer had built up such a close relationship with an official so highly placed in such a short period of time, but all I had done was ride along with some army lawyers on a couple of visits to his office. While there, I would chat him up, show a lot of interest in his anticorruption campaign, and placate his ego. Though I was a lawyer back home, I didn't serve as a lawyer in the army—but it turns out flattery works just as well on Afghan lawyers as it does on American ones, because by the time Sabet came to see me more as an intelligence officer than as a lawyer, we were already friends. He never turned down my requests for meetings.

Folks from other agencies were happy to take advantage of my connection to Sabet, so I received frequent requests to tag along with me when I'd go see him, including one time from a few guys from the Pentagon.

We pulled up to Sabet's little building in Kabul, were

let in through a haphazard gate, and came to a stop in his small courtyard surrounded by half-walls. Six men in Afghan Border Police uniforms greeted us with their AK-47s at the low ready position.

Kabul was a fairly long way from the border and Sabet had his own small security detail, so we weren't expecting to see border police. They started shouting instructions at us before we could even climb all the way out of our vehicle. "They're saying we have to leave our weapons and our body armor out here," said the translator.

The Pentagon fellas and I were dressed in civilian clothes—all amounting to some variation of cargo pants, baggy sweaters, and button-downs. All four of us (including the contract translator they'd brought along) had pistols holstered either on our hips or on the vests that held our body armor.

We each put our body armor into the vehicle, because it was rude to visit a contact dressed as though you thought he might blow you up. The next part was obvious, and the more experienced Pentagon gentlemen didn't need to tell me the proper move. Out of the sight of the border police goons, I pulled my 9-millimeter Beretta pistol from the holster on my body armor, stuck it into the waistband of my pants, and then pulled my sweater down to hide it.

We were ushered inside and into a little circular sitting area at the far end of a long room I'd never seen before. It resembled a courtroom, and for the next hour we watched

Sabet preside, listening to the pleas of Afghans who had traveled from all over the country.

It was like a one-man help desk. A man complained of corruption in Mazar-e Sharif, and another reported similar problems in Herat. Then a man and his wife stepped forward with what seemed like a workplace discrimination grievance concerning a local prosecutor in nearby Parwan Province. Apparently, the wife—her husband spoke for both of them—worked for a local prosecutor who was not allowing her to come to the office wearing her burka. Sabet would hear about each situation, write down a note, and then pass it to an aide, who would take the constituent into the next room where the aide would execute the orders Sabet had just noted on the piece of paper.

When the last constituent had been dispatched, Sabet came over to greet me, and I introduced him to my friends as we sat down for a visit. We made small talk for a few minutes about all the "cases" he had just handled, asked questions about several of them, and he told us about his process and what came next for all those people.

Eventually, an aide came in and handed him a note. He smiled at all of us and said, "I have a very good friend visiting me in Kabul today, and he'd like to join us and meet all of you." The border police goons came into the room and stood behind the chairs—still with AK-47s.

In walked a handsome man in the crispest, cleanest, most well-tailored Afghan Border Police uniform I'd ever seen. His beard was trimmed perfectly and he smiled a healthy-looking smile. He also looked very familiar to me.

"Jason, this is my dear friend General Hajji Zahir."

My throat went dry, but I extended my hand, shook his, and then, in Afghan tradition, we both placed our hands on our hearts. The Pentagon guys each shot me quick glances that said, "Holy crap, what the hell is happening?"

General Hajji Abdul Zahir Qadir was, at the time, someone the United States regarded as a high-value individual, meaning he was being watched closely. In that regard, he had experienced a bit of a fall from grace. His father had been a leader in the anti-Taliban northern alliance and was assassinated in 2002. The border police were very much a patronage organization, which is how Zahir became a general. Speculation at the time was that Zahir was working closely with the terrorist arm of the HIG, which—in addition to its sworn allegiance to al-Qaeda—was now affiliated with the Taliban as well.

It wasn't that Zahir had switched sides ideologically. It was suspected that he had sold out, and he was accused of running drugs and making a lot of money along the border. Zahir was considered to be among the most unscrupulous men in the Afghan government—which says a lot—and he was very possibly aiding the enemy.

This was a guy we were investigating and that US forces might soon be arresting or otherwise dealing with, and we were having tea with him. There was no way in hell he did not know that we were the very people who were investigating him. We acted as though we had no idea who he was, even though *we* knew that *he* knew that *we* knew exactly who he was.

Through the contract translator, Zahir told us about his exploits on the border, emphasizing how hard he was working at going after the warlords who were ruining Afghanistan with heroin. He said this with a smile. I had never seen anyone lie so comfortably and naturally—and with such joy. Now that I'm in politics, whenever I see someone do this, I think of Hajji Zahir.

I asked myself how much I trusted Sabet. In intelligence school, we had been taught to assess and predict three possible enemy courses of action: most likely; alternative (second most likely); and most dangerous.

Given that, I sized up the situation and decided that one of three things was happening:

1. Most likely: Sabet's friendship went back with Zahir to their days working for Hekmatyar,* or to their days growing up together in eastern Afghanistan, and Sabet was therefore totally ignorant of Zahir's latest exploits and really believed all this garbage Zahir was selling.

---

* Generally, there's a definite difference between the young politicians who worked in the HIG Party after the Soviet occupation and the terrorist group who swears allegiance to al-Qaeda and the Taliban today.

2. Alternative: Sabet's friendship had caused him to give his pal Zahir a pass—which was an act of corruption in and of itself—and he was doing Zahir a favor by giving him some face time with the people investigating him. A lawyer educating the jury pool—so to speak.

3. Most dangerous: I had drastically underestimated Sabet's personal ties to corruption, and the reason these goons were mean-mugging us was that if Zahir was unhappy with this conversation, we were going to find ourselves dead. Or kidnapped, then dead.

Just in case number three (most dangerous) was in play, I sized up the three goons and tried to determine how we might be able to get out of this alive even if that meant shooting our way out. There were four of us and—counting Zahir but not counting Sabet (he was a politician, not a fighter)—four of them. That left at least three more of Zahir's men out in the hallway or somewhere in the building, and therefore between us and our vehicle.

They had AKs and we had pistols, which wasn't great.

It was pretty clear that if things went bad, they'd know before we did, and they'd have the jump on us, so it was a dilemma, because the only way to survive option 3 was probably shooting first.

I decided I'd keep a close eye on the goons and the conversation, and at the first sign of a trap, I'd shoot first—I had already picked out my goon—and count on the Pentagon fellas to follow my lead. I also tried to ready myself mentally to follow a lead from one of the Pentagon guys if they saw something I didn't and decided to start shooting.

Knowing we needed to play along, we made conversation with Zahir about the goings-on at the border. He reported to us about all his successes out there arresting the bad guys. For quite a while, he went on about how the Americans didn't understand anything going on out east. He got quite animated explaining this point. I didn't feel like that was a great sign, and my heart started beating so fast I almost worried Zahir could hear my pulse.

After about forty-five minutes of nervous eye contact with his goons and half smiles at him, Zahir started dishing about warlords "the Americans must arrest if we want to slow the heroin trade."

Phew. I realized this was the moment Zahir had in mind when he asked Sabet to arrange this "chance" meeting, and now my heart could finally stop trying to escape my chest.

It seemed that Zahir figured we might ignore him if he gave us the goods on other warlords, but more than protecting himself, he was audaciously trying to use us to help his business model. It's a lot easier to corner the heroin market in eastern Afghanistan if the Americans arrest all your competitors.

We didn't care about the list of warlords he was laying out, because it wasn't new information, but we all feigned great interest in copying down all the names. Mostly we were just relieved to know we were probably going to get out of the room alive. The meeting ended a couple of minutes later with everyone—minus the goons—smiling and shaking hands.

When we got to our vehicle and opened the doors, I noticed all three of my colleagues reach inside to retrieve not just their body armor, but also their pistols.

To my shock, I was the only one of us who had been armed in there! I suppressed an urge to puke, thinking about how close we had come to getting waxed by my nearly taking the initiative and shooting first.

I quickly went from nauseous to pissed when I thought about the bizarre decision they'd made to go literally anywhere in Afghanistan unarmed. I just couldn't believe the Pentagon hadn't given them the same training we had been given. I stewed about it the whole drive back to Camp Eggers.

When I got back to the intel shed and told Colonel McCracken, my boss, that I had just had tea with Hajji Zahir, he laughed heartily and said, "Chinstrap,* we have weird jobs, huh?"

While writing this, I was curious about whether or not we good guys ever put Hajji Zahir out of business, so I googled him.

You'll be pleased to know he is currently a member of

---

* That's what he called me. I'll explain later.

the Afghan Parliament, so I am now of the strong belief he went legit and gave up any narco trafficking and ties to the enemy.*

To this day, Hajji Zahir is—by far—the most intimidating politician I've ever met.

———

Ron Richard was the Speaker of the Missouri House of Representatives during my first term in the legislature, and he never liked me much. Our relationship started off rough when he bounced me off a committee and I overheard his chief of staff say it was because Ron had political concerns about giving me too much of a platform. I told the press and they wrote about it, which the Speaker didn't appreciate. So during the first two weeks of my being elected to anything, he summoned me with explicit instructions relayed ahead of time: I was being given an opportunity to apologize.

The Speaker's secretary led me into his office and directed me to a seat at the end of a long cherry-red wooden table. He sat at the other end, about eight feet away from me. Three members of his staff dressed in dark suits stood behind his chair, crossing their arms and staring me down.

"I understand you have something you want to say to me," he said. This was my opportunity to say I was sorry, but I declined.

———

* Kidding about my strong belief. Not kidding about him being in Parliament.

17

"Mr. Speaker, you're a professional politician," I said, "and you made a political choice in how you were going to treat me, which I respect, but I'm a professional politician now, too, and I responded politically, so I'd expect you to respect that as well. I don't think either of us owes the other an apology, sir."

Ron disagreed and demanded one anyway. "If you get into a media battle with me," he said, "you'll be in a fight you can't win."

I'll admit, I wasn't thrilled to be picking a fight with the Speaker, and I didn't know how it would turn out for me, but at least I knew there was no chance I'd have to shoot my way out of his office.

"Mr. Speaker, I got here two weeks ago and no one knows who I am, so with all due respect, sir, if I get in a media battle with you, I've already won."

He audibled to his plan B and mentioned a bill I'd recently filed. "If you want so much as a hearing on it, you'll apologize right here and now," he said.

The Speaker was a tough old country boy for sure, but this was Jefferson City, not Kabul, and try as he might, Ron Richard was no Hajji Zahir.

"I appreciate your advice," I said. "As you know, the Associated Press wrote about that bill when I filed it, and I'm sure they'll be interested to know the Speaker of the House is holding a bipartisan military families bill hostage because a freshman hurt his feelings."

A few months later, my military families proposal became law.

Perspective is perishable, and it takes guts to preserve it.

Camp Eggers in Afghanistan wasn't very big. You could walk from one end to the other in about two or three minutes. The chow hall tent was right next to a little shack with five or six phones where anyone could go in and make a call home. Sometimes the line to get into the phone shack was pretty long, and there was a time limit on calls.

As often as I could, I'd go straight from breakfast to the phone shack. If I got there early enough, I could sometimes catch Diana before she went to sleep. If not, I'd still call, because she kept the phone next to the bed. During my deployment, she was half-asleep for about 60 percent of our conversations and would wake up in the mornings trying to figure out if we'd talked or if she'd dreamed it.

Right between the chow hall and the phone shack—beneath the ground—was a septic tank. But not like the kind of septic tank we're accustomed to here in America, where a hose hooks up to a small opening in the ground and pumps out the waste. The one next to the chow hall was just a hole in the ground, and every morning somebody had to open the hole, set a little fire, and burn all the feces in the open air.

So while I was in line to call Diana, human excrement floated in the atmosphere around my nostrils, a smell that never mixed well with my full stomach.

Whenever I'm having a rough morning getting my four-year-old son, True, ready for school or summoning the motivation to get to the gym for an early workout, I remind myself of the many times I blew my nose into a tissue and everything that came out was brown.*

I'd like to say this gives me a permanently healthy perspective that's kept me from having a "rough morning" ever since, but that wouldn't be true, because I sometimes forget how good I have it now.

For my first couple of weeks in Afghanistan I lived in a tent until—thankfully—I was allowed to move into a safe house where seventeen people shared two bathrooms.

The floors were all tile or wood and there was a thick layer of dust that covered every surface. I had five roommates, and the six of us were divided up into three sets of bunk beds in a little basement room that was approximately twelve feet by ten feet. The walls were covered with the decor put up by whoever had been in the room before any of us. It was mostly posters of sexy American female pop stars, but there was also quarterbacks Donovan McNabb and Brett Favre, and I thought of them as a partial historical record of the previous occupants' hometowns. I always

---

* Yep. You guessed it. Fecal soot.

wondered whether someone had brought all those posters with them or asked for them to be sent from home.

I really got to know only one of the guys I bunked with (his name is Heath), and he's still in the military and about to become a colonel. I remember a few conversations with the other guys, and I vaguely remember some faces, but Heath's is the only name I've retained from the group in our little sleeping cave. We all worked insane hours, and it was rare that you could have a conversation inside the room without waking someone up. With so many different schedules and no leisure time, one of us was always trying to get a few hours of sleep before returning to work. While there were six bunks in our room, I must have had about fifteen different roommates during my tour, because guys were constantly heading home or getting transferred elsewhere in Afghanistan.

To this day, I loathe getting dressed in the dark because it reminds me of that depressing little room. Every morning, I would try to suit up as quietly as possible in complete darkness, which is hard when you're still half-unconscious after just three or four hours of sleep. It's damn difficult to avoid making noise when getting dressed means putting on a ton of heavy equipment, some of which is made of metal or steel, and tiptoeing around uniforms, backpacks, duffel bags, and other gear we had to creatively arrange into piles in order to fit into our little basement corner of Afghan real estate.

Since nobody swept or vacuumed or cleaned at all, we

learned never to put on our boots or our uniforms without first checking for scorpions and camel spiders.*

Given my Afghanistan lodging situation and the numerous times in training when I'd slept in the woods as rain penetrated my poncho hooch, I make for a pretty low-maintenance houseguest.

Yet as that little basement room fades further into the rear view, I occasionally catch myself getting annoyed about stupid stuff—like a weak Wi-Fi signal or a broken air conditioner.

So while perspective is golden, it's not permanent, and it expires much faster when you neglect to question your own perception. In political terms, failing to maintain perspective is how someone loses touch.

Speaking of which, one of the very first decisions I ever made as a legislator was—in a roundabout way—whether to raise my own pay. It was early 2009 and the depths of the Great Recession. I had been in Jefferson City only a short time, but already—without my realizing it—I was falling prey to the pull of "inside the capitol" thinking.

Now, I never went in for the idea that I *deserved* a raise. In fact, I *knew* I didn't. Privately—and occasionally publicly—legislators would complain about the pay. They called it a "huge sacrifice," but we made $35,000 per year

---

* By the way, I got around enough to see how some other Americans in Afghanistan lived. A helluva lot of them would have considered my setup to be cushy as all get-out.

for just five months of full-time work, and we were free to work other jobs the other seven months of the year.

Many years ago in Missouri, an independent commission had been established to set salaries for judges and elected officials, but the two were also bound together, so that judges could receive a raise only if elected officials received one as well. I'm sure the idea was to give legislators political cover to increase their own pay, but it didn't work, because the legislature also had the option of voting down the salary increase. The result was a political incentive for legislators to say no to the money—something I'm sure the judges found irritating.

What warped my perspective was the argument from the state judges that *their* $90,000 per year starting salary was discouraging good people from serving on the bench. As a lawyer myself, I knew the quality of jurists in these positions mattered, and that we needed to recruit the very best, but the law said judges and legislators had to get raises at the same time, so it was all or nothing.

I, along with many others, wanted to separate the two pay increases so that we could give the judges theirs while turning down our own, but the law in Missouri made that impossible.

The morning of the vote, I called Diana from my office in the state capitol and told her that even though I didn't think we should get a salary increase during a recession, I felt like I had to vote for it because of the judges.

"Are you crazy?!" she asked. "You've gotta be kidding me!"

At first I defended my position, telling her this was just how things worked in Jefferson City.

She was home in Kansas City, outside the bubble of Jeff City politics, so she was totally unconvinced. "Your constituents are out of work! The economy is cratering. And frankly, the judges don't deserve more right now either. Are you seriously thinking about casting one of your first votes in favor of increasing your own pay? Do you have any idea how out of touch that sounds?"

That last bit of reality socked me upside the head. As has happened often, Diana reset my perspective and saved me from making a stupid decision.

I realized right then that if I was going to stay connected to life outside the bubble of elected politics, I couldn't be a wimp about it. Because of that conversation with Diana, I've never supported any measure that would give me a raise—and in fact I've worked against each proposal.

For years, I touted this part of my record as proof that I was "in touch with working people."

Then, one day during my Senate campaign, I realized that even though I was right to turn down the pay raises, the idea that it meant I was "in touch" was just a case of me buying my own bullshit. In a speech to workers at an iodine factory outside Kansas City, I brought up my opponent's record of voting to raise his own pay many times as a member of Congress while simultaneously opposing any increase in the minimum wage.

"I support an increase in the minimum wage and I've

never voted to increase my own pay, in fact I've always voted against my own raises. So you know I'm committed to—"

"You voted against your own raise?!" a man yelled from the third row.

"Many times," I said proudly.

He was incredulous. "Why would you do that?"

I hadn't anticipated this reaction. "You can't vote to increase your own pay," I reminded him, "so why should I be able to?"

We were approaching my salary from different perspectives, and he shook his head in bewilderment. "Man, if I could increase my own pay, I sure as hell would!" That got a laugh from the crowd. Then he really nailed me. "I don't know if I can trust a man without the good sense to accept a raise."

When I heard the choruses of "Uh-huh," "Damn right," and "I heard that," I knew I'd lost that particular audience.

I'm not sorry I voted against the pay raises. I'd do it again, but that was the last time I tried to brag about it.

Perspective isn't permanent, and if you're not strong enough to question yourself, you'll be the last to know you've lost it.

Politics is a profession practiced entirely by amateurs.

My favorite political parody scene takes place in the Mel Brooks classic *Blazing Saddles*. Governor William J. Lepetomane (played by Brooks) is seated at his desk, half-drunk and signing bills.

"One more bill for you to sign, sir," says an aide.

"What the hell is this?" the governor asks.

"This is the bill that will convert the state hospital for the insane into the William J. Lepetomane Memorial Gambling Casino for the Insane."

Governor Lepetomane hurriedly stumbles to his feet and holds the bill aloft.

"Gentlemen!" he says to an audience of sycophantic politicians. "This bill will be a giant step forward in the treatment of the insane gambler!"

His announcement is met with a chorus of harrumphs

and applause. Lepetomane adopts a hero's stance, putting one foot on a chair—inadvertently revealing that he's not wearing pants.

A secretary then reads aloud from an urgent telegram sent by the citizens of Rock Ridge. It reports the town to be living under a reign of terror, concluding, "Send new sheriff immediately."

"Holy underwear!" the governor declares. "Sheriff murdered? Innocent women and children blown to bits? We've gotta protect our phony-baloney jobs, gentlemen! We must do something about this immediately."

"Harrumph, harrumph, harrumph," goes the chorus. When the ruckus dies down, the governor points angrily at one man. "I didn't get a harrumph out of that guy."

An aide indignantly demands of the man, "Give the governor a harrumph!"

"Harrumph," says the man, looking shocked and afraid.

"You watch your ass," warns the governor.

Aaaaaaaand scene.*

I love how perfectly Brooks captures the false bravado and improvisational outrage politicians sometimes exhibit. As my great-uncle John, a Broadway composer,** likes to ask me about politics: "My goodness, is it all just theater?"

---

* My second-favorite political parody scene is in *The Campaign*, when Will Ferrell asks, "How's my hair?" and Jason Sudeikis replies, "Strong."
** Believe it or not, John Kander and Fred Ebb—not Frank Sinatra—wrote the song "New York, New York," as well as some of your favorite musicals, like *Cabaret*, *Chicago*, and several others. Given the bloodline, you'd think

I always tell him that the key to keeping my sanity has been to remember that everyone in politics, including me, is an amateur.

As a former political science major turned actual politician,* I'm here to tell you this ain't chemistry or physics, 'cause there ain't much science to it. It's a feel thing. There's no rule book for what works, which is why this is a book of lessons instead of rules.

As your fellow political amateur, I'll give you my opinion: politics is just how we all come together to make decisions about our communities and our country, and while there's plenty of good advice to be shared by highly experienced amateurs, there's no set path for success.

It's a profession practiced entirely by amateurs, and that means everyone can at least give it a try.

This ain't *The West Wing*. This is *Parks and Recreation*.

I loved *The West Wing*. Loved it. I've watched every episode more than once. We all wish it was an accurate representation of what it is to work in politics or government, and every once in a while I've had a moment that felt like

---

I'd have more rhythm or at least be able to play an instrument, but you'd be wrong.

* I challenge you to find a more toolish beginning to a sentence in this book.

it could have been scripted by Aaron Sorkin himself, but that's rare.

The benefit of us all being political amateurs, like Leslie Knope on *Parks and Rec*, is that sometimes the whole thing is pretty hilarious.

Which brings me to a story about strip clubs.

As the Missouri House of Representatives was debating a bill to more strictly govern conduct inside "sexually oriented businesses," the legislator at the microphone was speaking passionately, rattling off terms like "areola" and "anal cleavage." I was standing against the wall at the back of the chamber, talking baseball with a Republican staffer who was drinking an extra-large milk shake from a to-go cup.* I was talking up the Royals farm system and he—a Cardinals fan—looked bored and unconvinced.

The Republican staffer took a loud sip from his straw, grimaced a brain freeze away, and changed the subject. "Hey, I need a Democrat to do an amendment for me on this bill. Interested?"

"What's the amendment?" I asked.

"Nothing big," he said. "I just want to delay the effective date until December."

"Wait, didn't you help draft this bill?"

"Yeah," he said, "but I forgot to change the date, and

---

* Central Dairy's Jefferson City location was a short distance from the state capitol. On a warm day, you couldn't throw a bag of dark money in any direction without hitting a person drinking a milk shake paid for by lobbyists.

if anybody on my side offers the amendment, somebody might know I asked them to."

"Wait, let's back up," I said. "Why do you want to delay the law until December?"

"My bachelor party is in November."

"Uh, sorry," I said. "Can't help you there."

A focus on getting stuff done turns out to be pretty good politics.

I love baseball. I haven't played competitively since high school,* but one of the many lessons it taught me was how to be a "team-first guy."

Throughout Little League I was one of the biggest kids, which made me one of the best players on my team. By high school, the other kids had caught up to me in size, and that made a difference on the field.

For a couple of high school summers, I tried out for and made a premier team consisting of some of the best ballplayers my age in the Kansas City metro area. We were called the "New Yankees."**

We were a "traveling" team, which meant we spent most of the summer traveling around Missouri, Kansas,

---

* Diana says five days at Royals fantasy camp in January 2018 doesn't count.[1]
  [1] I disagree.
** A reference to our dominance, not a fondness of any kind for the actual Yankees.

Iowa, and Nebraska entering (and mostly winning) base-ball tournaments. We were all freshmen and sophomores in high school, but we would routinely beat varsity state championship teams.

Before those summers, I'd always batted leadoff and started games either on the mound or in center field, but I almost never made the starting lineup for the New Yankees. Coach used me as a pinch hitter, as a one- or two-inning relief pitcher, and as a late-inning defensive replacement in left or right field.

At first it hurt my pride quite a bit, but after a few weeks of watching my much more talented teammates, I realized I was lucky to have made the team at all, and I learned to think only about how I could do my job each game—whether it was driving in a couple of guys with a pinch-hit single or going in to get two crucial outs on the mound.

When I was a kid, the New Yankees taught me to worry less about playing time and more about impact. Years later, this perspective would help me answer the call of duty from my state by going to China and drinking more than I could handle.

In October 2011, Missouri governor Jay Nixon asked me to join his delegation for a trade mission to China. We spent about ten days in meetings with provincial governors and other high officials. Most took place over either lunch or dinner, and—as things apparently go in Chinese busi-ness meetings—all involved several rounds of drinking.

When it comes to alcohol, I'm a lightweight. I have a couple of beers every six or eight weeks, but that's it. And when I say "a couple of beers," I mean it literally. I drink two beers and end up with a slight buzz and an actual hangover the next morning.

Apparently wanting to keep his wits about him, the governor declared at the first meeting that I was his "designated drinker."

This helped him avoid seeming rude to our hosts, and he also got a good laugh out of everyone.

It was a solid joke, but the Chinese also took it literally, and I spent at least half of that trip intoxicated. I spent the other half hungover and sick. The morning of our last day in China, I walked in to the hotel lounge and sat down on a couch across from the governor. The Cardinals were in the World Series, and most of the governor's staff was from St. Louis, so the television had everyone's full attention.

At one point, the governor turned to me and broke the silence with, "Jason, you look like a hobo."

He was right. I really did. But I also felt good about having genuinely made a contribution to our efforts there, even if it wasn't in the way I'd anticipated. Odd as it may sound, the hobo line was basically him saying thank you. For the next several weeks after we got back to Missouri, every time he saw me he'd ask, "How are you feeling?"

He'd also tell me I did a great job in China.

In politics, putting the mission first sometimes means subjecting yourself to humiliation.*

Your dignity, unlike your integrity, is negotiable (for a good cause).

Mark Parkinson, a Republican state representative from the outer St. Louis suburbs, was never very nice to me, but I don't know if it was that he didn't like me, didn't respect me, or actually liked me a lot and didn't know any other way to interact than to behave like a first-grade girl kicking the boy she "hates" because she's actually sweet on him.

Look, it was confusing, but either way, the dude gave me a lot of attention.

Mark had a military-style haircut, high and tight; an NRA license plate; and he always smelled like cigarette smoke.

The best way to describe Mark to you is to say that he fit into this very small category of men who have always made me a little uncomfortable—mostly just because I can sense *their* incredible discomfort. Veterans reading this will know the type. These are the guys who haven't served but begin by telling you they totally would have but something or other beyond their control intervened. Then they'll tell you about their dad or uncle or brother

---

* And we haven't even talked about fund-raising yet!

or cousin or nephew or neighbor's kid who did something legitimately badass right before pulling out their phone to show you pictures of their guns.

Mark's passive-aggressive routine became more pronounced toward me when I left the House of Representatives and took office as secretary of state. He became kind of mean, and he also became the chairman of the Appropriations Committee on Administration, meaning he was in charge of the purse strings for each of the statewide elected offices, including mine. Knowing that my budget (and therefore our mission and our people's jobs) might be on the chopping block due to political animus, my chief of staff, Abe Rakov,* and I decided to mount a charm offensive with the committee.

I had a staff of 250 people, including a few who worked out of my capitol office a few doors down from Mark Parkinson's. Each statewide official had a capitol staff whose entire job was to deal with the legislature on our behalf. While some of the statewides (attorney general, lieutenant governor, etc.) did appear personally to present their

---

* This is a good time to introduce Abe; he'll be a recurring character in this book, as he has been in my life the last several years. He managed both of my statewide campaigns, served as my chief of staff and executive deputy secretary of state, and is now the executive director of Let America Vote. There's a great *West Wing* scene where President Bartlet is giving advice to a member of his cabinet and asks him if he has a best friend. The man says yes and Bartlet asks, "Is he smarter than you?" The cabinet secretary laughs and nods, to which Bartlet replies, "That's your chief of staff." That's also Abe.

budget requests to legislators before going up in front of Mark's whole committee, the others left these individual meetings up to their capitol staff.

Having just been a member of the house myself a few months earlier, I knew both the Republicans and the Democrats on the committee would see my following that usual practice as my thinking myself too cool for school. So Abe and I met with each member.

I had a nice office in the capitol and we brought them in one by one, yucked it up, ran quickly through our budget, and then gave each a thoughtful gift from the state archives.*

Having met with all of the committee members, it was time to visit the chairman. In a power move, Mark kept setting the meeting and rescheduling it. He also insisted that I come to him, which was pretty funny because the door to his office suite (which he shared with two other legislators) was just down the hall from our capitol office.

But what really had Abe riled up was a crude comment Mark's legislative assistant, Nick, had made to a member of our staff a few days earlier: "I can't wait for this meeting

---

* One of the secretary of state's many responsibilities is maintaining the state archives. Of course, we never gave away anything of value, but the staff was very good at making nice copies of old maps, pictures, or news articles with strong ties to each representative's district. Even the Republicans usually liked the gifts so much that they displayed them proudly in their offices. I'm a history nerd, so I loved this part of the job. I would sometimes pop into the state archivist's office on the first floor, sit down, and start a conversation with, "John, what's new in the past?"

to finally happen, because Kander is going to find out what my boss's balls taste like."

Abe, like a lot of people in his role, is more protective of his boss than he is of himself, so he was not happy about our having to demean ourselves in this meeting. From my vantage point of having known Mark longer, I was a little more able to see the humor in the situation.

On the day we were finally scheduled to meet, Jefferson City was hit by a blizzard. The roads were getting bad and there was speculation that the twenty-mile stretch of highway between Jefferson City and Columbia might be closed. I lived in Columbia. Mark knew this, so he had Nick keep calling us to say Mark was in a meeting that was running long. Abe and I waited in my capitol office and watched the snow fall for two hours. Between this and the ball-tasting comment, Abe was getting pretty irritated.

Finally, as the sun started to set and with the capitol totally empty of people, our policy director, John Scott, came in to tell us that Nick had called to let us know Mark was, at long last, ready for us.

When Abe and I entered the office suite, Mark's door was shut. Legislators almost never shut their doors, particularly when there are no people left in the building. Nick told us, "The representative is just finishing an important phone call."

The walls and doors were paper-thin. Given the silence in the room, it was obvious Mark wasn't on the phone, but this little act went on for a few minutes while we all stood waiting for the door to open. It was cramped; we were basically on top of one another, and it reminded me of being in an elevator. At one point, Mark called Nick on the office phone. In my four years as a legislator, I never once used the inner-office inter-com because it seemed silly when the person I wanted to con-tact was sitting ten feet away from me. Nick addressed Mark as "Sir" probably four times during a thirty-second conversa-tion, hung up, and told us it would be just another minute.

Nervously trying to chat us up, Nick asked Abe, "So what do you do for Jason?" Abe told him he was the chief of staff, and Nick began to explain that he did "a lot of chief-of-staff stuff for the representative" when the door swung open, Mark appeared, tossed a water bottle at Nick, and said, "Fill this up."

The office was almost as small as the one I'd had as a member of the house—not a reflection of Mark's standing, just a reality of the building. Between Mark's desk and the two small couches, there was very little space for anyone to move around. It was even smaller than the basement room I'd shared with Heath and the gang in Afghanistan.

Mark motioned for me to have a seat on the couch next to the window. It was a deep-cushioned, black pleather couch, and when I sat down, cigarette ash whooshed up into the air around me and settled on the pants and jacket of my blue suit. This was apparently where Mark sat when he blew smoke out the window. Given the smell, that's what he was doing while we'd been waiting outside his door.

I looked over at Abe and smiled. He gave me a look that said, "How the hell is it possible you're enjoying this?"

Mark immediately started needling me by bringing up Republican attack ads from the secretary of state's race, and I just smiled like it was all in good fun. When he ran out of confrontational small talk, he said, "I haven't bothered to read your budget proposal yet, so you'll have to go through the whole book from the beginning." It was about two inches thick, so I went right into it. Mark took out a tablet and, using a stylus as a pen, began taking notes.

Every time I moved in my seat, another cloud of ash was activated, so I repositioned myself on the couch, leaving my head touching one of the many enormous garments hanging from a mobile clothing rack next to the couch. "Those are my old suits," said Mark, who had lost something like two hundred pounds in the past year. "If you know any really fat people, let them know I've got suits here for sale."

Mark asked a ton of questions and appeared very interested in our budget. Each time I'd answer, he'd offer a skeptical-sounding "OK..." and make a note on his tablet. This happened several times and left me with the impression he was preparing quite an attack during the committee hearing, given the effort he was putting into obscuring the screen from view by either Abe or myself.

The whole process took about an hour, during which Mark seemed to have written a novel's worth of notes. As I stood to thank him and leave, he asked, "Wait a minute, where's my cool gift from the archives?"

Abe produced a framed copy of a grainy, black-and-white photo of legislators standing in the old state capitol in St. Charles, which was in Mark's district. "All right, cool," Mark said.

Just before we walked out the door, I caught a glimpse of the tablet lying faceup on the desk.

Mark had spent the meeting drawing a doodle of a bird.

I suppose one could describe this experience as undignified, but Mark didn't touch our budget in 2013, so it had all been worth it.

Every year of Mark's chairmanship, we'd walk out of that meeting and Abe would say, "That's the last time we ever do that," and every year we'd go through the routine all over again.

If all I have to do to advance the cause I care about is hand over a little of my dignity without compromising any of my integrity, I should do it, and I should make sure to take in all the details.

Because I'll enjoy telling the story later.

Lighten up.

During my time in uniform, the most commonly quoted line from the movie *Stripes** was "Aaaaaarmy training, sir!!!" It

---

* Starring the great Bill Murray as Private John Winger, *Stripes*—released the year I was born—is the *Citizen Kane* of movies that unfairly but uproariously portray the US Army as a bunch of incompetent fools.

was the standard mocking answer to anyone who—during an otherwise casual conversation—asked a question along the lines of, "What sort of training are we doing in the field this weekend?"

But my second-favorite quote from *Stripes* was "Lighten up, Francis."

It's during the movie's first act; basic training has just begun and the members of the platoon are in their barracks standing around their tough, grizzled old drill instructor, Sergeant Hulka. A trainee introduces himself as "Psycho" and threatens to kill anyone who touches him. His real name, he says, is Francis, "but any of you call me Francis, I'll kill ya."

Sergeant Hulka rolls his eyes and says, "Lighten up, Francis," and the whole platoon busts out laughing.

Oftentimes in politics, you just gotta remember to lighten up.

A couple of weeks after I announced my candidacy for secretary of state in 2011, I asked Governor Jay Nixon what advice he'd give me about running statewide. He thought for a moment and then said this:

"Wit is a powerful weapon in politics, but if you want to win a statewide race, aim that weapon at yourself as often as you aim it at others. Never be afraid to make fun of yourself."

I put that to good use. I've made plenty of mistakes, and I've usually been willing to laugh at myself and give everyone else license to laugh a bit, too. I mean, look, sometimes you're going to say or do something stupid— and the best thing you can do when someone calls you out on it is try to laugh along with them. It's a lot better than just letting them laugh *at you*.

Here's a trivial example of how this plays out, but instead of using myself as the subject, I'll tell you a story about someone else.*

Senator Roy Blunt, our opponent in the 2016 race, had held elected office in Missouri nine years longer than I'd been alive,** and had first gone to Washington during my sophomore year of high school. We consistently criticized him as someone who had become more Washington than Missouri. So when his campaign tweeted out a photo of a young man wearing a ball cap with a curly *W* volunteering at his campaign office, Abe tweeted jokingly that a Washington Nationals hat was the perfect attire to wear when volunteering for Senator Blunt.

One problem. The curly *W* on the hat didn't stand for Washington; it stood for Webster Groves, which is a suburb of St. Louis. Apparently the young man had come directly from his high school baseball practice.

Republican operatives were expressing feigned outrage all over social media, the high school kid posted a video about

---

* Pretty hypocritical of me, don't you think?
** Lucky duck probably saw *Stripes* on the big screen.

it, and Senator Blunt's son, former Missouri governor Matt Blunt, tweeted how "disappointed" he was that Abe had "disparaged" a fine young Cardinals fan. Right on cue, Missouri Republicans were harrumphing for each other all over the Internet. Believe it or not, in the era before Donald Trump was elected president, *this* really was considered a gaffe.

Reporters were calling Abe for a comment.

The communications team drafted an indignant, breathless statement in which Abe would take offense at anyone painting him as bullying a young volunteer and pivot into a criticism of Senator Blunt as a Washington insider.

I was on the road, but Abe called to tell me what was going on. After he read me the draft statement, I asked, "Is that how you really feel about this?"

"No," he said. "I stepped in it and they're making me pay for it fair and square."

"Why don't you just say that?"

So Abe put out this statement instead: "I've marched in the Webster Groves 4th of July parade enough times that I should have been able to tell my W's apart. This year, I'll be wearing one of their hats in the parade to make up for this mistake." And then he topped it off with a joke that proved he did know the local sports rivalries: "I apologize in advance to any Kirkwood fans."

The Republicans tried to get more mileage out of it, talking on and on about "Kander bullying high schoolers," but Abe's taking ownership of the whole thing let the air

out of the "scandal" and reporters never wrote a second round of stories about it.

Since we're on the subject of grown-ups picking on kids, let me up the ante and tell you about the time I took a hard line against disabled young people.

As a freshman representative in the minority party, my office was on the first floor and my desk was in the very front of the house chamber, which was on the third floor. We voted by pushing one of three small, square, adjacent buttons on our desks. Red (no); green (yes); or orange (present). I'd often do work in my office and listen to the live audio feed of the house debate, but it was always a couple of minutes delayed, so the bell signifying a vote could sometimes take me by surprise and send me sprinting up the stairs. I'd usually make it, but occasionally the vote would close as I was reaching for the buttons.

In 2009, when I was brand-new, I inadvertently made some news with one of my rushed votes. I was running through the back doors of the chamber, dodging other state reps, when I heard the Speaker ask if everyone had voted—the informal code for "going once"—so I picked up the pace. I was nearly to my desk when I heard him slowly say, "Mr. Clerk," the warning that meant, "going twice." Just as he began to say, "Please close the board and tally the vote" (Sold!), I lunged for the top of the little button box on my desk and aimed for the green "yes" with my thumb, but I missed and hit the red "no."

I looked up at the board. Every name was green but mine. Out of 163 state representatives, I had been the lone vote against a law requiring schools to accommodate disabled students who wished to participate in their own graduation ceremonies.

Aghast and confused, Republicans and Democrats alike kept asking, "What the hell, Kander?"

The most creative heckle was, "Bold stand, brother!"

Given the rather small constituency for what had apparently become my unforgiving opposition to our state's most inspiring high school graduates, I surmised this could be a political liability. If this happened to a member of Congress, they'd probably be asked about it right away and would have a chance to explain themselves, but nobody really cares enough to write a timely article about the vote of one state legislator on a noncontroversial bill that passed overwhelmingly.

So I walked back down to my office and wrote a tongue-in-cheek essay about the difficulties of being a freshman legislator with thumbs too big for last-second voting and sent it to my meager e-mail list.

Thankfully, someone at the *Kansas City Star* noticed my e-mail and ran it in the paper.

It wound up being one of the best-known and most popular things I did my entire first legislative session, and it was all because I leaned into it and made fun of myself rather than trying to spin it.

We have to get electricity out of politics.

It's easy to get distracted by cable news and social media, but in reality, the stuff that divides us is pretty thin, even if the only way to see that is to tune out the peripheral noise and focus on understanding one another. Politically, I learned that lesson because a blacksnake slithered across a transformer, fried it, and cut off all power to the state capitol in 2009 during an LGBT rights debate, marking my favorite day in the state legislature.

When the power went out, the Speaker wanted to account for every legislator (some were stuck in elevators), so he ordered all of us to sit in our assigned seats on the house floor. We were approaching the end of the session and he didn't want to waste any time, so he determined we would continue debating the matter at hand without the benefit of microphones.

Now, this was surreal, because usually the Missouri House of Representatives is like a cocktail party with a five-drink minimum. Everyone talks to one another while two representatives stand at opposing microphones and debate for the benefit of the press in the upper gallery— some of which the press can hear over the loud roar of the mingling representatives. This was just what had transpired in the regular course of business that morning prior to the power outage: opposing talking points traded back and forth, convincing no elected member of anything new.

But thanks to that snake giving its life for democracy,

we all had to sit there quietly so the two debating representatives could hear each other. This changed their tone dramatically and made the debate more respectful.

Suddenly, we were all listening.

Let me reiterate that this was an amendment having to do with discrimination against gay people.

In 2009.

In Missouri.

This was just two election cycles removed from the state voting 71 percent to 29 percent in favor of a constitutional amendment banning same-sex marriage.

And yet with all the usual distracting noise out of the way, people were listening. Thanks to the rays of sunlight coming through the stained-glass windows of the house chamber, I'll never forget the faces of my colleagues in those moments. I thought to myself that we should never turn the power back on, and I made a mental note to remember this moment because it would probably motor my faith in the process for the next several years.

After thirty minutes, the power came back, the roar reemerged, and the talking points returned, but I saved that mental image, and it did sustain me for a long time.

If you can push out the noise and get to a quiet place of rational conversation, it becomes clear we're just not that far apart from one another.

Play the hop. Don't let the hop play you.

When I was a kid, when Dad hit me grounders at baseball practice, he taught me to charge the ball rather than wait for it to make its way to me. "If you don't charge it, it's gonna hit a clump of dirt, take a bad hop, and get you all tied up, so just charge in on it."

"Play the hop," he'd say. "Don't let the hop play you."

On September 30, 2011, Missouri secretary of state Robin Carnahan, a Democrat, announced she would not seek reelection the following year. I knew this was a possibility, so I had already drafted an e-mail announcing that I would consider running, and for fifteen minutes I sat in front of the computer deciding whether to send it or to instead write a version announcing that I was full-on going for it. Diana had been a proponent of the second route, but she had told me she was all in for either approach. I quickly drafted the "I'm running" e-mail, saved it, and went back to staring at the "I'm considering" option.

Chris Koster, a fellow Democrat and then the Missouri attorney general, called me on my cell phone and spent five minutes hammering away at me to just go whole hog and send the second version.

"Jason, this business rewards the bold," he said. "If you are willing to put yourself out there and fail—to be publicly humiliated in front of all your friends and family—that makes you very dangerous to the status quo."

I could hear Dad in my head. *Charge the ball.*

Politics is a profession practiced entirely by amateurs.

I pulled up the "I'm running" version and hit Send.

A friend once told me I'd look back someday at that decision—which played a big role in helping me clear the field in the Democratic primary—and see it as the most pivotal moment in my political career, and perhaps they're right, but here's what strikes me about that: It wasn't a scene out of *The West Wing*; rather, it was a poorly dressed dude staring at a screen, talking to a "party elder" who gave sage advice but wasn't about to step in and clear the field like someone would on television or in the movies.

Because in a profession practiced entirely by amateurs, there is no umpire—there's just the sandlot.

The easier path isn't tempting because it's better; it's tempting because it's easier.

St. Louis is a four-hour drive from Kansas City. I'd been campaigning for secretary of state a mere three months, and already I'd stayed over at my colleague Representative Jill Schupp's house outside St. Louis so many times she and her husband, Mark, had taken to calling their spare bedroom "the Kander suite."

While I was tucking myself into bed at casa Schupp, a bipartisan redistricting commission in Jefferson City was wheeling and dealing* over the shape of state legislative

---

* Protecting incumbents. More on this in Lesson Number Six.

districts for the 2012 elections, but I hadn't been paying much attention to it.

Instead, I was trying to sleep without thinking about the poll numbers I'd been seeing lately. The Democratic brand in Missouri wasn't looking too healthy.

Meanwhile, I'd yet to fully clear the primary field, and I was grinding it out trying to raise money. It was early in the race, and I didn't even have a campaign manager yet. I wasn't having a high morale day.

My cell phone vibrated. The screen indicated it was a close friend who worked for the governor and who was monitoring redistricting machinations in Jefferson City. I answered and he immediately delivered more bad political news.

When I'd started running statewide a few months earlier, I came up with a backup plan. I had to give up my state representative seat to run, but if I lost the secretary of state's race, I could run for the state senate in 2014. My state senator, Jolie Justus, was a Democrat whom I supported, but she would be term-limited in 2014, so it would be an open seat and I'd be all but a shoo-in for the nomination in a heavily Democratic district.

According to my friend, a compromise had been made among the redistricting commissioners, making the Tenth Senate District—where I lived—the Seventh Senate District. The reason this mattered? Even-numbered districts held midterm elections, and odd-numbered districts held elections in presidential years, meaning the state senate seat where I lived would be on the ballot in 2012, not 2014.

Bye-bye, backup plan. Running for secretary of state had always meant walking a political high wire, but now it meant doing so without a net.

If I lost in 2012, which at that moment looked like the most likely scenario, there would be no apparent path back into elected office for several years. In my mind, I was picturing an actual cliff.

The phone call ended with my friend saying, "I'm really sorry, man, but I think the only move here is for you to drop out of the secretary of state's race and announce you're running for state senate right now."

The prospect of following his advice was downright seductive. At that moment, I had already raised about $400,000, which wasn't enormous for a statewide campaign, but more than enough to scare off any serious competition in a state senate race.

I could go home and relax for the rest of the year knowing I'd be moving up from the House to the Senate.

The most alluring feature of the whole thing, of course, was that I knew I would win the state senate race, and I had absolutely no idea if I had a chance in the secretary of state's race. The state senate race had that unmistakable quality of being "safe."

It was late, I was tired, and doing the easy thing instead of the right thing was looking pretty good. I was about to start talking myself into rationalizing this as the right decision when I decided to call Diana and tell her what was happening.

I had the phone on speaker, resting on my chest as I lay in bed, staring at the ceiling of Mark and Jill's spare bedroom.

I explained the situation with resignation in my voice, concluding, "So obviously we're going to end up running for state senate instead, right?"

She didn't hesitate. I remember every word she said: "You're just being weak right now. You're the one who's always told me you're not in this to be something, you're in it to do something. Well, here's your chance to prove it. You're not running *to be* secretary of state, you're running because if a Republican becomes secretary of state, they're going to take away people's right to vote, write biased ballot questions, and let the big banks* do whatever they want."

"Look, this is the big leagues," she continued, "and in the big leagues you don't get to know you're gonna win and you don't get a soft landing if you lose. Nothing has changed about the race other than you're scared. Too bad. Suck it up. I love you, honey, and one of the things I love about you is you're the guy who does the right thing even when it's hard. You didn't decide to run because you

---

* In Missouri, the secretary of state is the chief securities regulator.

thought you'd win; you decided to run because you knew it was the right thing to do."

She was right. Decision made.

Six months later I became the first millennial in the country elected to a statewide office.

Hustle and be humble.

Whether I had a good game or a bad game on the diamond, on the drive home my dad would often say the same thing: "You showed great hustle today." That's what Dad was all about. No matter whether we won or lost, the only thing that could ever make him disappointed in me was if I didn't run on and off the field or give it my full effort every single play.

One of the reasons Kansas City Royals third baseman George Brett became a hero to me was that I could tell he was a bit of a hero to my dad. We would sit in the stands at Royals games and watch Brett on every play. He was never out of position, never gave up on an at bat, and never gave anything less than his full effort. Brett wasn't fast—he was probably average speed for a major leaguer—but he made up for it with hustle.*

---

* Since 1950, only ten players had more inside-the-park home runs than Brett. In fact, Brett is tied for eleventh with Mickey Mantle. The Mick was a lot faster than George, but that's what hustle can do.

When Brett would hit a one-hopper back to the pitcher, Dad would point and say, "Watch, Jase, watch watch watch! See how he's running to first? He knows he's out, bud, but he's still digging as hard as he can!"

On former Royal Kevin Seitzer's first day in the big leagues, he saw it, too. That day, according to Seitzer, Brett "hit two one-hoppers to the pitcher and ran as hard as he could to first base. He set a great example for me to model my career. His hustle and desire—those were the little things that stood out for me."

I once saw an interview where someone asked Brett about the way he ran to first. He said he made it a game within the game. He'd see how close he could get to the bag before they threw him out. The next groundout, he was racing himself, trying to get closer than last time. For him, working his butt off was what made the game fun.

"I don't think I can play any other way but all out," he said. "I enjoy the game so much because I'm putting so much into it."

Brett still remembers the time he eased up on the gas for a split second. He put a great swing on a pitch, was sure he'd hit a home run, and jogged for half a second before going into a full sprint. The ball hit off the top of the wall, and Brett wound up at second with a double, scoring a run two batters later. This all happened in the fourth inning of a game the Royals went on to win, but here's how Brett—over two decades later—talked about his momentary lack of hustle: "It should have been a triple. It's one of the biggest regrets I have in my career."

Now, that's hustle.

Whether in the bleachers at Royals Stadium or on the Little League field, Dad wasn't just teaching me what hustle could do for me; he was teaching me the value of hustling for hustling's sake. It wasn't a means to an end. It was a virtue unto itself.

He wanted me to approach life the way Brett approached baseball. He wanted me to enjoy it because I put so much into it.

Army officers don't get hungry, thirsty, or tired, but they do sometimes choose to eat, drink, and sleep.

At Fort Lewis in 2004, I learned just how tired a person could actually be and still function. We'd been in the field immersed in a training exercise with real-world scenarios for a week, sleeping a couple of hours per night, conducting patrols in the summer heat all day, and now we were finally on the ten-kilometer march back to our barracks. I had sweat through my battle dress uniform and was feeling every pound of the water, ammunition, and rifle I was carrying. My Kevlar helmet and full rucksack were giving me a headache. Every time I closed my eyes for longer than a standard blink, I would find myself immediately going into REM sleep and I'd start having dreams.

But my legs just kept carrying me.

Once you've pushed yourself to work that hard, it's like a muscle memory of sorts. You always know you can go a little farther. I called on that muscle memory during intelligence school. I'm not much of a runner by army standards, and the sergeant first class in charge of training our platoon was very much a runner. Bad luck for me.

The US Army's intelligence school is at Fort Huachuca, Arizona, at the foot of the Huachuca Mountains. The fort itself is 4,623 feet above sea level, so if you don't like running, the thin air *literally* sucks. If, like me, you don't like the cold, I don't suggest going in the winter, because—as I learned—they would sometimes make us run in our summer PT uniforms—shorts and shirt sleeves—even when it was practically freezing with the windchill.

The signals intelligence folks do their schooling there, too, so there are huge radar antennae along "radar ridge." It's a pretty good hike, but I got used to our frequent runs up to the ridge and along it. The worst mornings were the ones when the sergeant first class in charge of our training was feeling fit, because he'd stand in front of the platoon before the sun came up—all of us shivering in the windy desert air—and announce: "I'm feeling good. We're running until our feet hit snow!"

It's Arizona. You have to run pretty dang high to find the snow.

As much as I hated it and as much as it hurt, I finished every one of those damn runs up the mountain. Once you learn what you're capable of, you run out of excuses for stopping short of your capacity.

When I came home from Afghanistan and ran for state representative,* no one thought I had a chance of winning. My opponents in the Democratic primary were well established and no one had any idea who I was, so I decided I needed to go meet everyone. I knew the biggest advantage I had was a willingness to absolutely work my ass off—to physically outpace the competition.

Diana and I identified the 8,000 homes most likely lived in by people who would cast a vote in the Democratic primary. Wearing the same boots I'd worn in Afghanistan, I set out to meet everyone behind all 8,000 doors. I knocked the entire list two and a half times, meaning I personally stood on a porch and knocked on a door 20,000 times over the course of that year.

Whether it was a hundred degrees or ten degrees, I was knocking. I trudged through deep snow, endured sunburns, and dodged dogs, but my feet just kept carrying me from one door to the next.

In the summer, Diana was often at the doors with me,**

---

* I warned you this book was unstuck in time!

** Probably five hundred times I watched in amazement as Diana laughed at the following corny joke as if it were the first time she'd heard it: "Where do you live?" a voter would ask, to which I'd reply, "On Ward Parkway, half a million dollars south of Gregory."

and in the winter she'd usually stay in the car entering data into the computer. I'd finish a block, she'd crack the window enough for me to slide in handwritten notes but not enough to let any heat out, and then we'd do it again at the end of the next block.

We put serious work hours into other areas besides door knocking, too. Diana made sure to log every note into a spreadsheet before she'd go to bed at night, sometimes staying up until three in the morning. She did so much data entry that after the campaign she saw a physical therapist for carpal tunnel.*

If I talked with someone and met his or her dog, Diana—along with Margaret Hansbrough, our one and only paid campaign aide—would record the name of the dog and I'd mention it in a handwritten note we'd send in the mail ("Say hi to Lucy for me!"). If they didn't come to the door, we'd log in something unique about their porch ("Sorry I missed you, but I love your Mizzou welcome mat!").

I hauled a backpack full of coffee mugs with my name on them, and I gave one to every person who came to the door. Before selfies were even a thing, I was carrying a digital camera and asking people to take a "mug shot" with me. Diana meticulously saved every little JPEG file by the name and address of the voter. With a week to go in the

---

* That wasn't the only injury. My mom knocked on so many doors with me that she ended up with knee problems. She was fully compensated in compliments, though, because half the voters would say, "What? No, you're too young to be his mom; you must be his sister!"

election, we sent one thousand households a personalized postcard with a picture of me and someone who lived in their house, both of us smiling and holding up a mug with my logo on the side.*

A year before the election, we started asking people if they'd host a yard sign the following summer. With two months to go, we delivered all of our signs over a single weekend. It got people's attention. You couldn't miss them when roughly one out of every four likely voting households had a Kander sign in the yard.

Two weeks out from the election, we replaced large signs with homemade ones in which we handwrote the homeowner's requested one-word answer to the question: "Why am I voting for Jason Kander?"

We even had life-size cardboard cutouts of me made. They featured yours truly holding a sign that read "I would really appreciate your vote," and we stationed them outside every polling place. I had met so many voters personally (and the cutouts were so lifelike) that several people accidentally walked up and started talking to the cardboard before embarrassedly realizing it wasn't the flesh-and-blood me.

People showed up at the polls drinking out of their coffee mugs and carrying their personalized postcard pictures of them and me.

---

* Years later Diana made a collage featuring hundreds of these little mug shots creatively arranged to form the logo of the Kansas City Royals. It's my favorite piece of art.

On primary day, I won a three-way race with 68 percent of the vote, but if I hadn't had the muscle memory of knowing what it was to work my ass off, I never would've stood a chance.

Work from the "have to" and wear your blinders.

Rookie of the Year, released in 1993, is the *Citizen Kane* of movies about middle school kids playing major-league baseball. In a freak accident, the film's twelve-year-old hero, Henry Rowengartner, develops the ability to throw a baseball over 100 mph. He signs as a pitcher with his hometown Chicago Cubs, and in one of his first outings he's too nervous to hit the strike zone. His hero, the team's ace pitcher, visits him on the mound and tells him to "deal from the have to."

Maybe not the best movie in the world, but I love that little morsel of wisdom. Basically, your "have to" controls your ability to perform when failing just isn't an option.

When you run for office, one of the most common questions you get from a reporter is some version of "Can you win?" I've always found this question overrated, because I'm not sure how it affects the decision a voter has in front of them: Should I vote for this person?

To me, asking a political candidate whether they can win is like standing over a drowning man and shouting, "Think you'll make it to the surface?"

Like the drowning man, a candidate can't waste time considering his or her chances of success, because everything in their power must be committed to achieving their goal.

To keep plugging away when there's no spotlight, you have to develop a strong "have to."

My "have to" worked overtime when I ran for secretary of state.

Ever hear of the index fund? Well, the guy who came up with the idea for that innovative way of investing across the market is a billionaire by the name of Rex Sinquefield. Rex lives in St. Louis, Missouri. He and his wife, Jeanne, are prolific philanthropists, but Rex's hobby, as far as I can tell, is collecting Missouri politicians.*

At first, he wasn't sinking his money into politicians. His political gateway drug was ballot initiatives. Rex is a true believer in radical conservative economic theory and he likes to use Missouri politics as his laboratory.

In Missouri, if you gather enough signatures from registered voters, you can send a constitutional amendment or change to state law to the ballot for a vote of the people. Because the requirements are pretty stringent, it's very difficult for citizen groups to actually get something on the

---

* Rex's other great passion is chess, which is—no kidding—why just about every elected Republican in Missouri has taken up the game in the past decade.

ballot without substantial financial backing from a rich person or interest.

Rex is a one-man interest group, and he spends millions of dollars trying to change the constitution or the law. He attempted to end the state's income tax by increasing the sales tax, wanted to eliminate earnings taxes in St. Louis and Kansas City, and also sought to apply his free market economic theories to public schools with programs like school vouchers.

When it comes to actually getting his ideas on the ballot, his success rate is pretty good. However, getting a majority of voters to vote yes has proved a lot harder. This is, in my opinion, due to the fact that Rex has bad ideas.

Rex disagrees and thinks his ideas are fantastic, but a few years ago he did figure out—after a few losses in a row—that Missouri voters don't share that opinion, so he apparently decided it'd be a lot easier to get them to vote yes if he himself could write the question that appears on their ballot. Or, if not technically write it himself, at least wield immense power over the person who does: the Missouri secretary of state.

Given that the governor can't veto a constitutional amendment, you can see why the race for the secretary of state's office is one of the most heavily contested in the state. Rex figured that he who forms the question shapes the answer, and Rex was tired of the answer coming back shaped like a big fat no.

Many Democratic politicians had sought to pacify Rex

by backing some of his policies and a few even earned his support with their capitulation. Others took the approach of pretending he didn't exist in the hopes he would leave them alone. No statewide candidate had ever tried taking Rex on by calling him out publicly.

Rex and I sat down for lunch during my campaign for secretary of state. I brought Abe and Rex brought his lobbyist, so there were four of us around the table. I'm sure Rex expected me to ask for support, but it was a waste of time for me to worry about what he was going to do, because I already knew he was going to support my Republican opponent.

Once we started eating, Rex and his lobbyist explained to me how it was that I was wrong about pretty much everything, but their demeanor was largely cordial, they kept their condescension to a minimum, and the food was decent, so I listened politely.

As lunch wrapped up, Rex steered the conversation in such a way that I was provided an opening to make a request, but I told him I hadn't come to ask him for anything.

"I know you're going to support the other guy, and that's your right," I said. "But I want to give you fair warning that I'm not going to hesitate to point out to Missourians why you're doing it."

I told him that as secretary of state I would write ballot language that was nonpartisan, clear, and totally unbiased, and that I was going to do that no matter what he chose to do in the campaign.

The skepticism on his face told me he thought I was bluffing about taking him on publicly and lying about playing it straight as the state's chief election official.

A few weeks later, Rex made his first financial foray into our race.

I was in the midst of "call time"* when Abe walked in and told me Rex had just given $250,000 to our Republican opponent. Honestly, that was pretty discouraging news. Our goal for the entire quarter was $250,000, and now, with one check, the Republicans had matched three full months of my fund-raising. Assuming our opponent even had to bother to pick up the phone to ask Rex for that money, he'd done in one call what I'd not yet achieved in thousands.

I looked down at the call sheet in front of me and stared at the phone number of a university professor in Columbia, Missouri, named David. My eyes scanned down to the "suggested ask amount": $250.

This was a gut-check moment.

I thought about my "have to" as I dialed the phone. David picked up and I made my pitch.

"Oh, jeez, I'm really sorry," he said. "I just can't do two-fifty right now, how about a hundred?"

"David," I said, "I don't mean to sound ungrateful at all, but Rex Sinquefield just gave Shane Schoeller** two

---

* Calling people on the phone and asking them for money (for the campaign—not for groceries or gambling debts or anything like that).
** Shane, the Speaker Pro Tem of the state house, was my Republican opponent.

hundred and fifty thousand. Do you think you can stretch out for the other hundred and fifty bucks?"

The other end of the line was silent for a moment, and then David laughed and said, "All right, how about I do $200?"

"That's $200 more than I had before I called you. Thank you!"

If not for that little victory, I'm not sure how I'd have felt, but it was enough encouragement to keep right on dialing.

If a racehorse didn't wear blinders, they wouldn't run their best race, because they'd be too distracted by the other horses. As a candidate, I tried to keep that fact in mind. All I could control was what I raised for my campaign, not what Shane raised for his. When donors would ask me if I could raise enough money to keep up with Shane, I'd say, "Yes, because I have to."

Abe and I kept our promise to go on offense against Rex. On October 19, the *New York Times* fronted its election page with a giant picture of Rex ominously surveying pieces on a chessboard. In a long article, Rex was exposed nationally as a cautionary tale about what American politics might look like if contribution limits were repealed nationwide. Follow-up stories appeared in Missouri's major newspapers, including some scathing editorials.

Rex didn't like the attention, so the final six-figure contribution he made to Shane was funneled through a PAC in Washington, DC, allowing Rex to conceal his identity until months after the election.

All in all, Rex spent almost $900,000 against me and was responsible for roughly 70 percent of Shane's campaign fund. I, on the other hand, kept my blinders on and just kept raising money a few bucks at a time. I even narrowly outraised Shane despite my biggest supporter accounting for just 4 percent of the $1.7 million I raised.*

And, most important, we won the race and I earned the responsibility of drafting ballot language for four years. Much to Rex's surprise, I kept my promise and wrote the questions fairly and without bias.

However, Rex's side still kept losing at the ballot box, because his ideas were just plain bad.

You can't buy hustle.

No matter how well we did at fund-raising, it was always possible for Rex to go digging through his couch cushions, pull out a few hundred thousand bucks, and eliminate our advantage, so we also hustled in another arena where we knew he couldn't catch up: mileage.

---

* I had an incredible campaign team, including when it came to fund-raising. We repeatedly called a farmer outside Rolla, Missouri, to ask him for $250, and he would always say, "Jason, we need some rain out here and then maybe I can help!" One day Kellyn Sloan—our call time manager— pulled up the weather radar on her computer and said, "Look! It's raining in Rolla!" When the farmer picked up the phone, I said, "Hey, it's Jason. It's raining!" "Nicely done," he said. "I'll get my checkbook."

Abe and I logged more than ninety thousand miles in his Ford Escape during that campaign, shaking hands and passing out flyers at nearly every town festival, VFW post, and county fair in the state.

On election night, we trailed in the returns until well after midnight. Even though we would go on to win by 40,000, that first lead was only 2,800 votes. When that result popped up on Abe's laptop, I looked at him and said, "County fairs."

He nodded and smiled, because we both knew we'd shaken at least that many hands at county fairs alone.

In politics, hustle is the only equalizer, because big money can catch up immediately in every category but hustle.

If I've put in the hustle—knocked on the doors, built the relationships, logged the miles—it's physically impossible for someone to catch up in a short period of time. The other side can run a last-minute blitz of negative ads, but they can't go back and replicate a year's worth of ground game.*

Well-meaning friends and supporters will caution, "Things are looking good, so ease up a little. It's a marathon, not a sprint." Whenever someone said that to me, I'd suggest they go to YouTube and type "marathoner celebrated too early" into the search field.

---

* Good thing Rex invented the index fund and not the time machine.

Besides, I've always figured I'm a lot more likely to win if I sprint the whole marathon.

Strongly consider the possibility you might be wrong.

My mom is a badass.* She grew up in foster care, was sent to a reform school for girls despite never really misbehaving, put herself through college, ran a group home at the age of twenty-one, became a juvenile probation officer who disarmed big kids with knives, and then raised me, my younger brother, Jeff, and a whole bunch of other boys she all but adopted into our home.

At my wedding, her toast was a poem she had written to all of us titled, "boys boys boys."

She didn't care about sports at all, but she did care about us. To this day, I doubt Mom could explain a force-out, a touchback, or a technical, but she came to every baseball, football, and basketball game I ever played.

She was always super encouraging and never questioned anything we said or did on the field, so she got our attention the one time she challenged our thinking about baseball.

Driving my "foster" brother Mel and me home from seventh-grade baseball practice, she posed a hypothetical

---

* To the outside world. To her kids and grandkids, she is always warm and loving.

question. "How would you boys feel about it if a girl played on your team?"

"What? Mom, that's crazy," I said.

"Why is it crazy?" she asked. "If she's good enough to make the team, why wouldn't you want her?"

We thought about that for a moment before Mel answered for both of us: "It's just tradition I guess. Girls don't play baseball."

"Yeah," I said, "tradition."

She pulled the minivan over to the shoulder of the highway, reached across Mel in the passenger seat, and opened his door. "I guess y'all better walk home then," she said.

Mel's eyes were as big as saucers and I'm sure mine were, too. "Mom, what are you doing?!" I asked, thinking she'd lost her mind.

"It's tradition," she said with a smile. "Girls don't drive."

Mom's bluff worked, because we sure did think about it the whole rest of the way home, which is why this story about gender equality is also one of the first times I learned to consider the possibility that I could be totally wrong about something I was completely sure of.

Afghan attorney general Sabet's mother may never have taught him that lesson.

Sabet had enemies throughout Afghanistan and within the government, and by the time he and I met, he had been the target of numerous assassination attempts.

I mentioned earlier that folks from other agencies liked to tag along with me on my Sabet visits. I'd have needed to check with most Afghan government contacts before bringing a new person, but Sabet liked unannounced new people because it gave him a chance to show off. Karen was an FBI agent, and she joined me because she was working on several investigations she thought might benefit from a conversation with Sabet.

Afghans don't have the same rigid sense of time as Americans, so schedules are more like guidelines than rules, and it was common for Sabet's previous appointments to stick around and be a part of my visits with him. On this day, we were joined by a prosecutor who worked for Sabet in one of the eastern provinces.

Sabet was, as usual, in Western dress—though this was uncommon for Afghan government officials in my experience. He wore a well-tailored gray suit and sported a long, untrimmed gray beard. A tall, thin man, he looked sort of folded in half as he sat on a low-to-the-ground, thoroughly used couch and leaned out over his knees to drink his tea or pick raisins out of a bowl on the table.

Within the first few minutes of the visit, Sabet informed Karen and myself that we should feel free to speak candidly because his guest, the provincial prosecutor, did not speak a word of English.

The prosecutor was dressed in a heavily worn suit with no tie. He had bad teeth and his complexion lacked the healthy color of Sabet's. He looked like many of the people in the rural Afghan provinces—or at least he looked like the ones who were not warlords.

Karen was sitting directly across from Sabet on a mismatched but somewhat similar couch. I was in a wooden chair facing toward both of them, sort of at the head of the small coffee table. The prosecutor shared a couch with Sabet, seated on his right. After some small talk, we got pretty deep into the topic of Sabet's anticorruption efforts with a particular focus on corrupt Afghan National Police commanders. I scribbled in my notepad as fast as I could.

The anticorruption campaign was the easiest topic to get Sabet to discuss, but the hard part was steering the conversation toward details and away from anecdotes about Sabet successfully taking on the bad guys. The anecdotes made for good listening but held little intelligence value. Had they been US Army stories, they would have started, "So, no shit, there I was..."

The moral of each of these stories was that Sabet was impressively brave and immensely important. Karen, who was doing a masterful job of playing into his desire to impress a new American guest, asked him if he thought he might run for president.

"The people want me to," he said. "But Afghanistan is not like America. In Afghanistan, you have to be a rich man to win an election."

The prosecutor had been silent this entire time—smiling amiably but doing nothing to indicate he understood any of the conversation. Sabet riffed about corruption suspects in the very province where this gentleman was assigned and noticed Karen and I glance at each other.

Without gesturing or indicating in any way with his body language that he was talking about the prosecutor, Sabet said, "In fact this man is part of the problem and is terribly corrupt."

I fought the urge to look over at the man, and, in my periphery, I could tell he just kept smiling the same unknowing smile.

"If he is corrupt, why not fire him?" asked Karen.

"Politically impossible, so I watch him closely," he answered. Sabet casually sipped his tea and added, "In fact, this man sitting next to me has been directly involved in several plots to kill me, but thankfully he is totally incompetent."

As he said this, he let out a morbid laugh, which Karen and I met with nervous smiles. Wanting to communicate he understood a joke was told, the prosecutor smiled, too.

We continued the discussion—switching to other provinces—long enough that Karen excused herself and stepped outside for a cigarette. While she was gone, the prosecutor turned to Sabet, said something in Dari or Pashto (I couldn't tell the difference), shook my hand, and left.

"He has another meeting," Sabet told me.

A few minutes later, as Sabet and I were wrapping up, Karen returned looking a little rattled. We bid Sabet our good-byes, thanked him for his time, and promised to visit again soon.

When we got back in the vehicle, Karen told me that

while she was outside smoking, the prosecutor stopped to have a smoke, too. After standing together in silence for a few moments, he asked her—in barely accented English— where she was from and told her about the farmland he owned in Nebraska.

Whether in Afghan or American politics, it's always a good idea to consider the possibility your assumptions are dangerously wrong.

In 2009, state representative Jason Smith learned this lesson with far less than his life on the line.

When I first got to Jefferson City, the house Republican majority had yet to become a supermajority, so they couldn't override the Democratic governor's veto without at least twenty Democratic votes. That September—during the annual "veto session"—they were desperate to find *something* (*anything!*) so politically treacherous for Democrats that we'd throw our own governor under the bus.

Months earlier, President Obama and a Democratic Congress had enacted the American Recovery and Reinvestment Act—broadly known as the federal stimulus—as a response to the Great Recession. The Missouri General Assembly then passed a bill—sponsored by Republican representative Jason Smith—establishing a system to monitor how Missouri's portion of the funds was spent. They had done so in the name of fiscal responsibility, they said, and I'm pretty sure I and just about everyone else voted for the bill.

Then the governor vetoed it, which sounds like a pretty

dumb veto until you hear the governor's stated reason: The new bill created a new system without repealing the old one, meaning that instead of using the perfectly fine accountability system that existed under the law, we would now have a second, mostly redundant way to track the funds.

The result would have been wasteful and confusing, and, in my opinion, the governor's office made a good case for the veto.

But in politics, the simpler explanation (Republicans want to be fiscally responsible and the governor wants to use this money without anyone looking over his shoulder) often beats out the truth (it's fiscally responsible to use the perfectly decent system we already have rather than create a new one for no reason).

A waste of tax dollars or not, the Republicans were already dreaming about unseating the governor in three years with negative ads claiming, "When Barack Obama–loving liberal Jay Nixon tried to waste your money, even his own party said 'no way, Jay!'"

The governor could afford to lose only nineteen of us Democrats, so he was working the phones, and it wasn't going well, because legislators knew that voting with the governor could lead to similar ads against them the very next year.

The override attempt was expected to be a big success and a pretty serious embarrassment to a Democratic governor who had gone out of his way to cultivate his image as a responsible steward of the state budget. Conventional political wisdom "in the building"* was unanimous: this was a sharp strategy by the Republicans.

Two days before the veto session, I happened to see Governor Nixon at an event and we talked privately for a few minutes. He already knew he had my vote, so he asked me if I had any ideas for how to save his veto.

I told him I hadn't thought about it yet, and he asked me if I would personally get to work conceiving a strategy. Given that I was just a freshman legislator, I was surprised to be so directly asked to draw up the winning play. *He really is completely out of options,* I thought.

Recalling Sabet's dangerous overconfidence, I decided to take advantage of Jason Smith's certainty about the override. After all, the mind of everyone "in the building" was made up about how this was about to go down, so no one had their guard up.

Smith, a Republican from a bright red district, was well liked by legislators in both parties, and the last thing he was expecting was an ambush. Since he barely knew me from a hole in the ground, I might be able to make him believe I was just another friendly Democrat willing to help screw the governor.

I figured my best chance was to embarrass poor Jason

---

* An oft-used Jefferson City phrase referring to the state capitol building and encompassing everyone from elected officials to staffers to lobbyists. Longtime Jefferson City denizens are fond of touting their total years "in the building" as evidence of their wisdom.

Smith so badly that anyone who voted for the override would wind up being embarrassed, too, and I knew Smith was so bullish on his chances that he wouldn't be humble enough to hustle, so he wouldn't stay up late doing his homework. The night before we debated the bill I made sure to stay up late and do mine.

When my turn at the microphone came the next morning, I asked permission to "inquire of the bill handler," which meant I wanted to ask Smith some questions. The Speaker asked Smith if he would accept my request and he did, so I had fifteen uninterrupted minutes to question him on the bill.

Using a kind and casual tone, I began by telling Smith I was troubled by the governor's claims that this bill was unneeded and that I'd love to get Smith's help in clarifying some of the provisions in his bill. He relaxed immediately.

I then read word for word off the papers in my hand, stopping at the end of each legislative provision with a softball question. For instance, I'd read a line to him and say, "Now, this seems reasonable to me. What are you trying to do in this part of the bill?" or, "Would you say this section makes our system more fiscally responsible?"

I really leaned into the act of turning on the governor by asking stuff like, "What in the world was Governor Nixon thinking when he vetoed this?"

This routine lasted about ten minutes. Since I seemed to be double-crossing a governor of my own party, everyone had stopped their side conversations. Once I had everyone at rapt attention, I thanked Smith for being so helpful, turned back toward the front of the chamber, and said, "Mr. Speaker, I'd like to speak on the motion to override."

When the Speaker told me to proceed, everyone was really leaning in, thinking a freshman Democrat was about to tear into the Democratic governor.

"Mr. Speaker, the gentleman from Dent County did a fantastic job answering my questions. In fact, I am absolutely convinced the bill I read off to him is desperately needed in this state. But there is one problem, Mr. Speaker. Unfortunately, none of what I just read to Representative Smith was from his bill. Not one word. And while it's pretty bad that he has no idea what's in his own bill, it's actually much worse that he can't tell the difference between his bill and the one passed several years ago to oversee the spending of these funds. The governor has argued that we shouldn't pass this bill because the system as it exists is all we need, and now we know he's right. The Republicans want to pass this bill to embarrass the governor, but the only thing embarrassing about this is the fact that they have no idea what they're doing."

Representative Smith* was pretty sore with me for a year or so, but thanks to his hubris, and a little hustle of my own, we upheld every single one of the governor's 2009 vetoes.

---

* Now Congressman Smith.

The surest way to be right about something is to discover you used to be wrong.

Missouri, like most state governments, balances its budget every year to satisfy a requirement in the state constitution. This "balanced budget amendment" didn't always work out perfectly in Missouri, but it did at least force some conversations in the legislature about raising revenue in order to afford the cost of education, health care, and infrastructure.

Given that context, I thought a balanced budget amendment at the federal level might be a way to force Congress to end subsidies for oil companies and tax breaks for corporations that ship jobs overseas, so I supported it.

Once I saw the budget President Trump proposed in 2017, I had to take a hard look at my support of a balanced budget amendment and decided I had been wrong. With the way things are in Washington these days, this Republican Congress would never have the gumption to raise revenue or cut corporate giveaways. I should have seen this before, but I didn't, and while that's a little embarrassing, I'm glad the army taught me to always consider the possibility I might be wrong.

I realize now that a balanced budget amendment at the federal level wouldn't make Congress set the proper priorities; rather, it would just encourage a bunch of political scaredy-cats to first save their donors, and the American people would get the raw end of the deal.

Hustle and be humble.

The difference between politicians and everyone else is not that politicians never think they're wrong; it's just that they're afraid to admit it. When hubris gets you in trouble, humility gets you out.

I was wrong. It happens to all of us, and we shouldn't be afraid of recognizing it.

Never lose your inner chinstrap.

I've had a lot of nicknames.

Growing up, I was called Face by my friends after the member of the A-Team who always talked the group in and out of trouble. In the army, as I went through training, I was Kondor (I have a big nose); Kan-Do (I liked that one); and Too-Kan (because both I and the Toucan bird have big noses).

But by far the most elaborate nickname I've ever received came from Colonel Jack McCracken, the US director of intelligence in Afghanistan at the time of my deployment.

Let's break down this positively regal nickname.

Before I'd ever even met him, Colonel McCracken nicknamed me "Kandahar." He'd seen my name on a piece of paper as an incoming soldier and thought it similar enough to the southern Afghan province. But that was only the beginning.

The intelligence division was a joint unit, meaning it was made up of people from multiple military branches. At that moment in time, it had absorbed a big chunk of a Navy Reserve intelligence unit from California, so it was heavy on navy personnel.

It was a little odd to have a unit in Afghanistan that had more navy folks than army folks, so Colonel McCracken jokingly took to referring to my rank by its navy equivalent. Second Lieutenant Kandahar became Ensign Kandahar.

Pretty boring so far, but my run-in with a senior officer *earned* me the last part of my nickname.

Having just returned to Camp Eggers from a trip outside the wire and dressed in full battle rattle, including my Kevlar helmet, I was walking toward the intel shed. My hat—which we refer to as a soft cap—was in my right cargo pocket.

I made a stop on the way to my unit's building and was given some paperwork. I didn't have a free hand to carry my helmet, so I had a choice to make, because "headgear" or a "cover"* is a mandatory part of the uniform. Instead of switching to my soft cap, I put my helmet back on my head, but it was a short distance to the intel shed and I didn't bother to snap my chinstrap.

About twenty paces from the intelligence shed, I saw a colonel walking toward me. Other than a pistol in a shoulder holster, he didn't have on any equipment and his

---

* More army words that mean "hat" but take much longer to say.

uniform looked nice and clean. A step behind him and to his left—as per protocol—walked two first lieutenants from his staff. Their uniforms looked just as clean and carefree as the colonel's.

I saluted, greeted him with a "Hooah, sir," and kept walking. Knowing I was "out of uniform," I winced as you do when you look down to check your speedometer after passing a state trooper on the highway.

"Stop right there, Lieutenant." I turned around to face him. I figured he was about to say something about my chinstrap, which he would be right to do, and that I would fasten it, render a salute, and we'd march back out of each other's lives forever. That's not quite what happened.

"What's wrong with your chin?"

That was my cue to set my paperwork and equipment on the ground and use both hands to button my chinstrap, which I did while answering him with a "Roger, sir."

I stood at attention waiting for him to dismiss me, but he just stared at me. Then he shot a "Watch this" smirk to his two minions before asking me something I didn't think people bothered to ask anymore.

"You active or reserve?"

"I'm a reservist, sir."

He sneered, nodded, and asked, "Do you know how I knew you must be reserve?"

I was still at attention. "Negative, sir."

"I knew you were reserve because no one from an active duty unit would ever do something as stupid as walk around here without their chinstrap fastened." He was now standing with his nose just a few inches from mine. "You're a disgrace," he said.

This was 2006. His characterization made no sense. We were long past the days—if they ever existed—where you could tell the difference between active and reserve soldiers in a place like Afghanistan. I mean, at that point, even I'd been on active duty for most of the past year.

On the inside, I said, "Sir, I don't recall you expressing such a negative view of reservists to the reserve brigadier general who visited Camp Eggers last week."

On the inside. On the outside, I just kept my eyes forward and my shoulders back. To be fair, he probably had no idea I'd been one of the low-ranking wallflowers in that meeting. Besides, talking back to him would get me nowhere, because the rank insignia on my uniform was a "butterbar,"* and his was a "full bird." Not to mention the most important fact: even though he was a jerk, he wasn't wrong about my being out of uniform, and he was actually just reinforcing the old saying, "If you can't get a soldier to button his chinstrap, how are you going to get him to die for his country?" The ethic behind it is that we enforce discipline all the time because discipline and consistency save lives.**

So all I said was, "Roger. Understood, sir."

---

* A derogatory term for a newly commissioned officer, "butterbar" is a reference to the single gold bar worn by a second lieutenant.

** Ironically, I later became a platoon trainer in Officer Candidate School, a job that required me to enforce uniform standards with extreme tightassedness.

With the minions laughing and him feeling pretty big, he was satisfied with the exchange. "Carry on, Lieutenant," he said.

I saluted, he saluted back, and I picked up my stuff and moved out smartly.

I was irritated, but not overly so. I told the story to a few of the people I worked with who were all fellow reservists, and they got me all spun up and angry. We sort of egged one another on. They convinced me to write an e-mail about it to my boss, Colonel McCracken.

Acknowledging the appropriateness of an on-the-spot correction about the unsnapped chinstrap, my note to Colonel McCracken took issue only with this other colonel's derogatory comments about reserve units.

Looking back, I can see that part of my e-mail was pretty sanctimonious. Pointing out to Colonel McCracken that his own intelligence division currently had more reservists than active duty personnel, I included statistics about how many reservists had been killed or injured since 9/11. And if that wasn't self-righteous enough, I even quoted Winston Churchill's "The reservist is twice the citizen."

A day later, Colonel McCracken casually called me into his office. "Kandahar, you were wrong, you know that, but he was out of line, too," he said. Then added, "I'll say something to him."

"Thank you, sir."

"Also, I'm definitely calling you Chinstrap from now on," he said. "Short for Ensign Chinstrap Kandahar, of course."

"Of course, sir."

I took it as a compliment.

For the rest of my deployment, he referred to me pretty much exclusively as Chinstrap. Later, he decided "Ensign Chinstrap Kandahar" sounded like something from an impressive lineage with a rich family history, so he added "the Third" to the end.

The day I left our camp for the last time to go home, I had a chance to address the unit, as was our tradition for folks rotating back to the States. Colonel McCracken introduced me, offered some nice compliments about the work I'd done, and then said, "OK, Chinstrap, take it away," but before I could talk he interjected, "Oh, by the way, you've all been working with him awhile and you may not know this, but Ensign Chinstrap Kandahar the Third is—fun fact!—actually Second Lieutenant Jason Kander."

During my campaign for the Senate, Colonel McCracken, who had since retired, recorded an ad for me, in which he faced the camera and said: "In the army, we don't care if you're a Democrat or a Republican. We just want to know that you're going to be there when the going gets tough. I was Jason Kander's commanding officer in Afghanistan. His work in army intelligence saved lives and he always chose the toughest assignments. We need that kind of courage in Washington again. Now political attack ads are trying to make Jason into something he's not. He's a Soldier. And he's the kind of change we need in the Senate."

It was a good and, I think, an effective commercial, but I so admire Colonel McCracken that the mere knowledge he was willing to vouch for me genuinely made me proud. Once the ad went up on the air, I got an e-mail from Mark Putnam—my media consultant—letting me know the colonel had insisted on making an alternative version just for me. I clicked on the attachment and played the video. It was the exact same ad but with the colonel—totally straight-faced—referring to himself as "Chinstrap Kandahar's commanding officer" and assuring the voters the attack ads "were trying to make Chinstrap into something he's not."

To me, that nickname is like a shorthand for the idealism that too often fades with age. I've learned a lot in the years since I got home, but I've held on to my ideals—even if I've sometimes balanced them with practical experience. This moment in American politics lends itself to hard-hearted practicality bordering on cynicism. Hope and optimism aren't always in vogue, but I don't want to eliminate my inner Chinstrap, because the kid who wrote that silly e-mail quoting Churchill is still a big part of who I am inside, and I rather prefer it that way.

Oh, and the other colonel in this story—the one who hated reservists—has also retired and entered the civilian workforce. I know this because his request to connect with me on LinkedIn sat in my in-box unanswered for about four years.

The secret to adulthood.

When I was in first grade, I committed a crime.

Mrs. Schubert had placed a yellow cupcake decorated with a single gumdrop on each of our desks to celebrate a student's birthday, and when I walked by Lauren Brandenburg's desk, I snatched the gumdrop from atop her cupcake, popped it in my mouth, and kept walking. It was red, my favorite color, and I'd acted on impulse.

Lauren noticed her cupcake was not like the others and notified the authorities. Mrs. Schubert launched an immediate inquiry, but the advanced forensic investigation technology we take for granted today wasn't available in the late 1980s, and no one had witnessed my crime.

I was home free.

If no one came forward, Mrs. Schubert announced, then the party would be called off. As she gathered the cupcakes into a tin, several sets of tiny shoulders slumped with disappointment, and the guilt got to be too much for me.

I started crying, which I knew had blown my cover, so I walked to the front of the room and—barely able to speak while sobbing—copped to the caper. It's remarkable how viscerally I still remember the Gumdrop Heist of 1988.

I was just a little kid riddled with guilt, but my mind was actively searching for a way to justify sustaining my silence. Eventually, this inner turmoil became so upsetting it literally poured out of my tear ducts.

With each passing year of childhood, I became more and more aware of right vs. wrong. By my teenage years, I rarely failed to know the difference, so most tough decisions were just a matter of weighing whether to do the right thing or the easier, wrong thing instead.

The only other time I've intentionally stolen something* was a weak moment in middle school. My close friends had been shoplifting candy bars from a local department store. They kept daring me to do the same to prove I wasn't too chicken and I eventually caved.

I knew it was wrong, but I told myself the store made plenty of money and so taking one thing just to fit in was barely even stealing.

I went in, wandered around, saw no one around me in the apparel section, grabbed a tie,** stuffed it in my shoe, and ran out without being caught.

I never did it again, but I didn't return the tie either, because I had developed the standard human ability to justify my doing the wrong thing.

As we journey into becoming adults, we tell ourselves the following lie: it's just not as simple as right and wrong.

We say things like, "It's a bit of a moral gray area," or "There's a lot of right choices here," or "Sometimes you

---

* Intent matters! (This footnote is for every coworker who has ever let me borrow their phone charger.)
** Was I destined to be a nerd or what?

have to do something wrong for a really good reason." There exists a kernel of truth to all this because adulthood does present more moral dilemmas than childhood.

But for the most part, the rules we're now trying to teach our kids still apply to us, so, in my experience, here's the secret to adulthood: about 1 percent of our toughest decisions are made hard by our genuinely not knowing what constitutes the right thing to do, and the other 99 percent are just us deciding whether or not to do what we know is right.*

Being a good person doesn't change much between your first day of grade school and your first day of work.

Since that sounds simple, corny, and a little preachy, let me follow it up with a bold and controversial statement: being good at politics is not much different than being a good person, because if you do what you believe is right and say what you truly believe, people will be a lot more likely to keep you around.

When I said this on Bill Maher's show in early 2017, Bill responded, "Boy, you really are a Boy Scout!" and got a big laugh from the crowd.**

---

* I've been saying this for years believing it was an original thought of my own, but I recently came across this quotation from General Norman Schwarzkopf: "The truth of the matter is that you always know the right thing to do. The hard part is doing it." Given that I read the general's memoir when I was a kid, I'm pretty sure the third thing I stole in my life was when I swiped this axiom from Stormin' Normin and made it my own.

** I actually washed out of Cub Scouts at Webelo.

The best politicians don't make the best political decisions; they make the right decisions—absent of politics—and have enough game to handle the political consequences. "Professional politics" isn't the part where you make a decision; it's the part where you defend one.

If something feels wrong, it probably is, and if that something is your job, get a new one.

I didn't go to Afghanistan with a unit the way most people deploy. Instead, I went to fill a position within another unit. So when I came home, I wasn't part of a big powering down or any formal process; I just hung around the house for a week or so and then went back to work at my law office.

As a professional day-to-day, it was a little jarring.*

In keeping with the "secret to adulthood" being that you almost always know what's right and what's not, one case—between our corporate client and a local owner of a small business—stood out in the first few months after I returned. Prior to my deployment, I doubt the events in this story would have had such an effect on me, but after I returned home, I was keenly aware of how comparably meaningless and unfulfilling it felt to spend my days representing corporate America.

We had a hearing coming up on a motion that, if we

---

* Stay tuned for more on this later.

prevailed, would essentially win the entire case for our client. It was a long-shot legal argument, but as a matter of practice, it had to be made. Since we had little chance of winning the motion, the partner handling the case saw it as a good opportunity to get the rookie some at bats and decided to let me handle the hearing all by my lonesome. Knowing the client would appreciate a bill made up of only my hourly rate—a third of the partner's rate—he even went so far as to let me go to court totally unsupervised.

During the argument, I felt as though I was winning, but I had almost nothing to compare it to, so once it was over, I just packed up my accordion file and followed the other side's lawyer to the elevator.

I was pondering a scenic route back to the office—first-year associates rarely get outdoors during the workday. When the elevator doors closed, the other lawyer turned to me and said, "If you ever decide to leave your firm for a place that lets you loose in the courtroom, I hope you'll consider coming to work with us."

That seemed like a good sign. When I recounted the entire story to the partner an hour later, he smiled amiably and then reminded me we had practically no chance to win the motion. He promised to find more opportunities for me to go to court without much risk to the client.*

---

* There's no villain in this story. The partner was and is a good man who sought to give his clients the best representation he could and who genuinely wanted to mentor me and help me grow as a lawyer.

About a week later, the partner poked his head into my office sporting a happy look of disbelief. "Not sure how this is possible, but you must have said something that judge liked, because he just ruled in our favor," he said.

For about twenty minutes, I felt great. It feels good to win and impress your boss. Later, as I packed my bag and shut off my computer for the day, I could only think about the small business owner. How much he owed his lawyers, how much he was going to have to pay to comply with the judge's order, even what it would be like when he went home that night to tell his wife about the ruling.

By the time I got off the metro bus near our house in south Kansas City, I was positively depressed about it. That night, lying in bed with Diana, I unloaded all the misgivings I'd been having about my job. When I began talking about the small business owner, I got a little choked up.

She tried to be supportive by telling me it was his own fault and all I had done was my job. She wanted to absolve me of responsibility for doing what I was paid to do.

"As a lawyer, what I did was right," I said, "but it's not what a soldier would do."

I knew she understood when she said, "No, honey, it wasn't. I'm sorry."

When I started at the firm, I was a lawyer who did soldier stuff on weekends, but I had come home from Afghanistan a soldier who happened to do lawyer stuff on weekdays.

Not long after that conversation, the same partner came

into my office again. He wanted to talk about something I was writing for another corporate client. I hadn't taken the assignment as seriously as the firm and the client deserved, so he said something totally reasonable like "This is really important."

I replied by asking, "Is anybody gonna die?"

He didn't get mad. He just sort of assumed I regretted the question and let it go, but in that moment we both probably knew I wasn't in corporate law for the long haul.

Around this same time, I went to a continuing legal education seminar and listened to a plaintiff's lawyer named Tim Dollar speak passionately about his work representing individuals who had been injured by corporate negligence. In every case, he said, he worked not just to win money for his clients, but also to force corporate defendants to change practices and prevent future tragedies.

Tim's passion gave me goose bumps. Over the next two nights, I reread *The Rainmaker* by John Grisham and started getting pretty excited about the world of plaintiff's trial law, but I was still unsure about leaving the security of my big firm with its big salary and its free bagels and doughnuts on Friday mornings.

I needed some mentorship, and I knew just who to call.

When I was fifteen years old, my dad met a lawyer named Sly James who made such an impression on him that Dad asked Mr. James to mentor his kid who thought he might want to be a lawyer when he grew up. I'm not sure why Sly said yes, but I'm glad he did.

Sly—a marine and the first African American partner at Kansas City's biggest corporate law firm—gave it all up at the height of his career to open his own plaintiff's firm and represent individuals. I called Sly to get his take on whether I could do the same even though I had yet to establish myself at all.

"What should I do?" I asked after explaining the situation.

Sly presented me with a clear choice. "Jason, there's a lot of good reasons to stay where you are. It's a great firm, they'll train you well, and you've got a chance to make a lot of money. In a few years, they'll even let you handle your own clients and try your own cases. You'll be pretty good at it, you'll win a big one, and then the following Monday you'll come into work and the partner in charge of your department will tell you the client is unhappy with the bill."

"Or?" I asked, already smiling because I could see where Sly was going.

"Or you can leave, go to a plaintiff's firm, start representing real people and trying cases right away, and probably make a whole lot less money over the course of your career. But it won't be long before you have a car accident case where you get an insurance company to pay your client $25,000, and when you call to tell your client about it, they'll start crying because you will have changed their life forever."

Sly paused for effect, then nonchalantly added, "Your call, kid. Do what you think is right."

I put in my two weeks and left to become a plaintiff's trial lawyer working out of a converted McDonald's on the other side of town.

Turned out that job was pretty terrible, but it did lead me to eventually practicing at the Barnes Law Firm (me, another guy, and a guy named Ken Barnes) and—thanks to Ken—getting to do all the stuff Sly had described.

Doing the right thing is a seriously underrated political strategy.

I eventually got to repay Sly for all he'd done for me when, years later, he—who had never run for office—announced he would challenge the sitting Kansas City mayor in his reelection bid. This was after I'd been elected to the State House, so when I became the first elected official to endorse Sly's campaign, everyone I knew had three questions for me:

1. "You know every KC mayor has been reelected since before the Great Depression, right?"
2. "Who the heck is Sly James?"
3. "Wait, he's a black trial lawyer named Sly, and you think he's going to win?"

Not only did he win, but I think he's the best damn mayor in America, and so does Kansas City, which is why he was reelected with 87 percent of the vote four years later.

It was a risk to leave the firm and it was a risk to go all in for Sly. It felt risky at the time, but it also felt right. Even if neither had worked out the way I intended, it wouldn't have changed the fact that both actions were the right choice for me, and that's the secret to adulthood: keeping it as simple as doing what's right.

In the final scene of the movie *Bleed for This*, an interviewer asks boxer Vinny Pazienza, "What was the biggest lie you were ever told?" to which he responds, "It's not that simple."

"Why not?" she asks.

"No," he says, "that's the biggest lie I was ever told: it's not that simple."

"And what's the truth?" she asks.

"That it is."

Never ask anyone to do what you won't.

In 2009, Missouri Democrats were trying to extend health-care benefits to more of our state's children, and because this was a year before Obamacare defined the issue, several members of the Republican majority were willing to break with their party leaders and support a plan put forward by Governor Nixon. Unfortunately, not quite enough Republican members would take this stand. No matter how many different ways we proposed amending the budget to pay for it, we kept coming up just a few votes short of extending health care to more kids.

What I found most frustrating about it was the hypocrisy, because as state legislators, all of us enjoyed excellent health benefits at the taxpayers' expense. In my mind, too many of my colleagues were asking the children of low-income families to endure something to which we ourselves would never even consider subjecting our own loved ones.

It reminded me of the time I tried to get out of climbing the rappel tower. Since enlisting, I'd had to rappel, climb up towers, and occasionally ride in helicopters with the door open. I hated every second of it.*

As a platoon trainer for Army Officer Candidate School, I had to supervise my officer candidates as they mastered height obstacles on the confidence course at Fort Leonard Wood. The first time through, I managed to supervise from the ground. However, my commanding officer, a major, saw what I was up to and confronted me about it. I pointed out that I'd already done all this stuff back when I was going through training.

"Yeah, but you're still asking your soldiers to do something you're no longer willing to do yourself."

He was right and I was wrong, which was why I complied when he suggested I enroll in the rappelling instructor certification course. I spent a lot of time hanging off

---

* How severe is my fear of heights? I don't even like being this tall.

that awful tower, and my soldiers could tell I was afraid, but they respected the fact that I was up there with them.

I had been trained never to ask anyone to do something I wasn't willing to do, but on that day, my CO had to remind me.

With that lesson in mind, I offered an amendment to the budget that would spend the money necessary to give health-care benefits to more of Missouri's poorest children, and—this is the kicker—pay for it by cutting money used to pay for state legislators' health care plans. I was calling the majority party out for asking our constituents to do something they weren't willing to do themselves.

At first, the Republicans were hopping mad at me and angrily smashed the red "no" buttons on their desks. But then someone on their side of the chamber realized a bunch of "no" votes would play in the paper for what it was: a bunch of Republicans taking care of themselves at the expense of poor kids. The Republican "whip team" walked up and down their side of the aisle, convincing members to change their votes from no to yes.

By the time the vote was complete, my amendment had passed the house with overwhelming bipartisan support.

Don't be a spotlight ranger of decency.

United States Army Rangers are some of the toughest, most elite soldiers in the world. To become a Ranger, you have to graduate from a grueling sixty-one-day combat leadership course. Rangers are the best of the best. I was not a Ranger.*

"Spotlight Ranger" is army slang for someone who appears to be an outstanding soldier and a team player when the boss is looking, but half-asses it and refuses to contribute the rest of the time. No one likes a "Spotlight Ranger."

When I was a cadet coming up through officer training, we'd have the occasional spotlight ranger within our ranks and it irritated all of us to no end, but once I became a Platoon Trainer for Officer Candidate School I realized Spotlight Rangers only *think* they're fooling the boss. We could always tell.

Spotlight Rangers are as rare in the army as they are common in politics. But in politics, it's not just people who won't put in the work, it's more commonly an Eddie Haskell**–like divide between the public and private persona.

It is entirely *possible* for politicians and high-profile-type people to slow down and show respect. The good ones— the ones who aren't just Spotlight Rangers of decency—do it whether there's a camera present or not.

On Election Day 2006, Diana was volunteering for then state auditor Claire McCaskill's campaign for the US Senate. She was working in a field office, helping to coordinate teams of get-out-the-vote canvassers. It was a toss-up race,

---

* I'm guessing you didn't need me to clarify that.
** A butt-kisser of the highest order.

and Claire was leaving it all out on the field, hitting every corner of the state.

The door opened to the tiny little office and Diana looked up to see the candidate herself come in and make a beeline right for the desk where she had been organizing clipboards.

Diana and I had done some local organizing and been around her a little, but Diana would not have bet much money on Claire knowing our names.

With no cameras and no crowd, Claire gave Diana a hug, leaned in close to her, and said, "Diana, I so appreciate that you're here helping me. I've been up for thirty hours straight, I don't know which way is up, and I'm nervous as hell, but whenever I'm tempted to feel sorry for myself, I think about the fact that Jason's over there in Afghanistan and you're here. I just want to thank you both. Please give him my love."

Then she turned around, headed back out the door, and went right back to campaigning.

If you look closely, you can see that certain politicians show that exact spirit all the time. Elizabeth Warren—while campaigning for me in Kansas City in 2016—learned that we had filled the 1,100-person venue and another 400 people were about to be turned away outside. She took me by the arm and led me downstairs, out the front doors, and in front of the 400 people in line.

With no microphone, she projected a shorter version of

the speech she was about to give inside, and then introduced me so that I could do the same. As we walked back upstairs, she said, "It's cold out there and those people waited in line over an hour!"

In that same campaign, I was sitting with Joe Biden in the back of his Secret Service limousine when he saw a fire station, ordered the motorcade to pull off, and brought me along with him as he thanked a bunch of very surprised firefighters.

While campaigning with me in Ferguson, Cory Booker nearly missed his plane home because he was spending time talking to a man who had recently been released from prison and was struggling to find work.

The caricatures of politicians as self-centered and interested only in the trappings of power don't always ring true. I dropped by Kamala Harris's office just to hang out and chat in the summer of 2017. We'd been talking for forty-five minutes before I realized there was nothing at all on her walls. She'd been a senator for more than six months and hadn't bothered to even hang up her diploma.

When I asked why, she said, "Oh, I thought I was going to do that right away, but there's too much important work to be done. Every time I get ready to decorate I just think about how trivial that seems when I could be helping someone."

That's not some cornball thing she made up for TV. That was just a candid conversation with a friend.

The tenor of this book might suggest to you that I think

all politicians other than myself are Spotlight Rangers of decency. I just want to make it clear that there are some really great people in this line of work, and I've mentioned only a fraction of them. If there's someone out there you are inclined to put a lot of faith in, I hope this book only deepens that inclination.

Those who give respect get respect.

My dad probably threw me—no joke—a hundred thousand pop-ups in our front yard, donating his right shoulder to making me a better center fielder. He sacrificed his knees and his back to making me a better pitcher by spending hours in a catcher's squat.

Despite all he'd put into my athletic abilities, it's a home run I gave up that taught me the most about what kind of man he wanted me to be. In the eighth grade, I threw Grady Wisdom—a kid from my school who played on another team—a curveball that didn't curve and Grady hit it very far. I walked over to the third baseline and shook Grady's hand as he completed his home-run trot.

At the time, I thought nothing of it. It was just my way of saying, "Good job. You got me this time," to a friend I knew I'd see at school on Monday.

But on the drive home after the game, Dad said, "When you shook that kid's hand...You've never done anything on a baseball field that made me more proud to be your dad."

The stuff we remember from childhood can seem almost random. Now that I'm a dad, I'm keenly aware that there's no way to know when I'm about to say something—good or bad—that my son, True, will never forget. I hope I do as good a job in those moments as my parents did, because in that moment Dad taught me about getting over myself and treating everyone with respect.

———

I knew May 4, 2012, my thirty-first birthday, was off to a rough start when a dog bit me on the hand. The Missouri House of Representatives was honoring the family of a fallen service member, including a German shepherd named Sergeant, the bomb-sniffing dog who had been with him in Afghanistan. After the ceremony, I spoke with the widow in the side gallery for a few moments. As she was telling me about her husband, I went to put a hand on her shoulder, but before I could, Sergeant intervened.

I felt terrible because the widow—on what was already a difficult and emotional day for her—felt embarrassed by it, so I just hid my bleeding hand behind my back. "I'm sure it's fine, don't worry," I said. "It's not Sergeant's fault," I assured her. "He smelled an officer and understandably didn't trust me."

That semi-inside military joke got her to laugh a little and, I hope, made her feel better.

But the day only got worse from there, because a few hours later the Missouri legislature overrode the governor's veto of a grossly partisan, blatantly gerrymandered congressional redistricting map. Needless to say, I was mad at the three Democrats who voted with the Republicans to make the difference, one of whom was Penny Hubbard from St. Louis.

Penny's husband and son had both held her seat before her. Since arriving in Jefferson City, she had made several deals with the Republicans and a lot of Democrats had written her off, including me.

When Penny got up to speak in caucus that evening, I think it may have been the first time I'd heard her voice. She scolded us, pointing out that most of us had just assumed her vote was gone and neglected to even speak to her about it. In fact, she said, most of us had never even spoken to her at all.

She laid into us good.

Most of my colleagues were so dug in that they just rolled their eyes, but I knew she was right. When caucus adjourned, I walked over to Penny, kneeled down by her chair, and shook her hand (with my left, undamaged paw).

"Penny, I'm embarrassed about the fact that we've never really met," I said. "I want to fix that right now. From here on out, I promise to show you the respect you deserve."

Penny and I had a few more conversations during that legislative session, but nothing substantial enough that I remember the subject.

Several months later, I was standing in front of the St. Louis City Democratic Committee as the Democratic candidate for secretary of state. Each of the candidates who had spoken before me had been raked over the coals. There was a lot of anger toward the statewide ticket—at least from the St. Louis City Dems' perspective—about an inadequate commitment of resources toward field operations in the city.

I explained that my campaign had limited resources, but that I would do all I could, and I assured them it was important to me. Just as the tough questioning started, state representative Penny Hubbard—one of four Hubbards on the committee—stood and addressed the room (which was in the Hubbard Community Center).

"I've served in the legislature with Jason," she said. "He is a good man. His word is good. If he says he's going to make us a top priority, that's what he's going to do. I'm vouching for him."

No one else had any questions.

Back when Penny made her deal with the Republicans, I could have railed against her and set fire to a bridge I'd never built in the first place, but what was done was done. And, most importantly, I had realized it was at least partially my own fault.

I'm not saying I've never been dismissive or disrespectful of someone I disagree with, because there's no doubt I've been guilty of it,* but I am saying I've at least *tried* not to burn bridges when all it would do was make me feel better.

---

* See: Twitter.com/JasonKander.

And, more often than not, I've tried to disagree in a way that's respectful. Sometimes respect is all people are really looking for from you. It takes a little everyday courage to acknowledge that and do the right thing, but it's worth it.

Every time someone comes through for me simply because I took the time to treat them with respect, I think of a scene from the Adam Sandler movie *Billy Madison*.* At the climax of the film, Billy's nemesis, Eric (portrayed by Bradley Whitford in his greatest cinematic role), pulls out a gun and is about to shoot Billy.

Just before he can pull the trigger, someone shoots Eric in the ass and saves Billy's life. The camera cuts to Steve Buscemi in the balcony with a rifle, smiling and waving to Billy. Earlier in the movie, Billy had called Buscemi's character on the phone to apologize for bullying him in high school.

The camera cuts back to Billy, who looks straight into it and says, "Man, I'm glad I called that guy."

---

* The *Citizen Kane* of movies about grown men retaking grades K through 12.

Keep it real.

You probably wouldn't have bought this book if you hadn't at least heard of me, and you might think you know me from a television appearance, or from Let America Vote, or from my podcast, or even just as a guy you follow on social media, but that's not how you first learned of me.

I first showed up on your radar because of a campaign ad in which I assembled a rifle, blindfolded, while making the case for gun control, and the best way for me to illustrate my point about the danger of playing political pretend is to tell you the story behind that ad.

I have an F rating from the NRA.* In fact, the NRA hates me so much that when I ran for the Senate, Wayne LaPierre, the president of the NRA, came to Missouri himself to personally campaign against me—while they were running millions of dollars in attack ads.

---

* Proudly.

To call Missouri a pro-gun state would be an understatement. In Missouri, a nineteen-year-old man can carry a gun nearly anywhere he wants without ever having to get a permit of any kind. In fact, if he bought it at a gun show, he doesn't even have to fill out the paperwork for a background check.

If he feels threatened by an unarmed person, he can shoot them dead and never spend a day in jail.

So when millionaire Lapierre's jet touched down in my state, my supporters got worried. All of a sudden everyone was calling the campaign, trying to convince me to do one of those ads where I shoot a really big gun, talk about how much I love hunting, and basically pretend to be a Republican.

I haven't been hunting since I was a kid, and, frankly, I didn't get into politics to play a character on TV, so I never considered going that direction. Instead, as a proud progressive running for Senate in a red state, I knew the best strategy would just be to keep it real.

"I bet I can put a rifle together a lot faster than the other guy," I said to my team, prompting them to ask if I could do it blindfolded. Since I had cleaned my weapon in the woods in the middle of the night so many times in the army, I told them I probably could. A few days later, Diana used her iPhone to film me as I sat on the living room floor, closed my eyes, and assembled a rifle I'd borrowed from my dad.

I texted the video to Abe and he shared it with the team who, apparently, lost their minds with excitement.

The resulting ad was me saying I was right about

background checks, the NRA was wrong, and I knew what the heck I was talking about. Most people agreed with me, and even if they didn't, they knew I was going to stand up for what I believed in, even if it meant going head-to-head with the NRA.

And while we may not have won the race, we did win the argument about background checks, because after that ad, the NRA pulled theirs down and retreated back to Washington.

In fact, we outperformed every other Democrat on the ballot in Missouri in 2016, including one who was endorsed by the NRA. It worked because we didn't think about the political calculations first—I did what I thought was right and then I defended my true beliefs.*

I've run statewide twice in Missouri. I won the first time and then, in 2016, just barely lost, but I overperformed the presidential ticket by 16 points. About 220,000 people who voted for Donald Trump also voted for me—more than any other competitive race in the country in 2016. And I didn't do it by pretending to be a conservative Democrat.

Everyone in my state knew I was a progressive, but they also knew I was saying what I believed instead of just pretending I agreed with them on everything.

When a politician takes a position because of seeing a

---

* Today I'm a member of the board for Giffords, and this footnote is a shameless plug for you to support the important work of Gabby Giffords and Mark Kelly at Giffords.org.

poll and not because it's consistent with that politician's true opinion, they're making a choice to *act* as though they believe what the voters believe. It's not politics; it's playing a character on television and trying to fool voters. But chances are, you're not a good actor.* I mean, if you were good enough at acting to make a living from it, wouldn't that be your day job?

From Hulu to Netflix to television to the movies, Americans don't just see a lot of acting—we see a lot of *good* acting. We so seldom see bad acting that when we do see it, it doesn't look like bad acting to us, it just looks weird.

And it makes us uncomfortable.

When a politician says everything you want to hear, but in a contrived bad-acting kind of way, you give them no credit for sharing your views.

I, for one, don't know how to act, so I don't try, but I understand why a lot of people in politics don't feel entirely comfortable being their true selves in front of an audience (or an electorate). It's natural to be a little shy and to resist being left so vulnerable to criticism, but that's why it takes nerve to keep it real in politics.**

---

* A good deal of Lesson Number Five is addressed to budding political candidates, but most everything in this chapter is applicable to anyone who seeks to persuade someone else.

** I once asked a politically active friend of mine who makes his living as an actor whether he'd ever thought about actually running for office, to which he replied, "Oh, no way. I love acting, but I don't want to act *that* much!"

Keep it real.

When you don't know, say so.

When someone has all the juicy gossip yet never asks a question, my antenna goes up. How can they know so much without ever asking anyone a question? I assume they're just making it all up.

I had already been a platoon trainer in Officer Candidate School for several months when a new captain got to our unit and immediately became my boss. I was a first lieutenant at the time and therefore his subordinate. Fresh off commanding a company in Iraq, he could have started giving me orders right away. Instead, he approached the job the first few weeks as though he worked for me.

He didn't speak directly to the officer candidates often; instead, he just watched and asked me questions off to the side about my choices so that he could learn from them. He eventually became an excellent platoon trainer and assumed the more traditional role of leadership.

Even though I remained a more experienced trainer, I never had any problem looking to him for guidance or following his orders. He made solid decisions and provided mentorship. He gave himself the chance to succeed because he didn't show up pretending that he had everything figured out in his new job.

In a funny twist, the night of one of the Officer Candidate School graduations, several of the new lieutenants told me that they were initially scared to death of that captain

because he never spoke. They figured he was quietly direct-
ing all of my actions!

The best leaders I encountered in the army all had in
common the fact that they never pretended to know more
than they did. They asked a lot of questions of those above
and below them in the chain of command and usually
wound up knowing more than their peers.

Their actions taught me the importance of being un-
afraid to invoke three powerful words: "I don't know."

When Michael Brown was killed in Ferguson in 2014,
a lot of Missouri politicians decided not to engage directly.
The sense I got from most of them was that they felt they
didn't have any good answers and so were unwilling to go
somewhere and address people who were certain to have a
lot of questions.

Within a few days of the incident, I was in Ferguson
asking as many questions as I could. I went directly from
an NAACP march to the Ferguson police chief's office for
a sit-down meeting. I spent the entire day asking questions
of everyone who would talk to me and when someone
demanded answers I would frequently say, "I don't know."

People were surprised at that, but not because they
expected me to know. They were surprised I admitted it,
and most reacted by helping me learn the answers. Those
conversations led to my starting #FergusonRebuild, a nonprofit effort that helped several small businesses recover
from damage during the unrest. I ended up spending more

time in Ferguson carrying out my official duties as secretary of state than in any other city in Missouri, because that's where I was most needed. If I had pretended I'd known what to do from the start, no one would have believed me, and I never would have been able to make any difference at all.

I prefer those who honestly disagree with me to those who dishonestly "agree."

Joe Ortwerth lobbied for the far religious right. A former Republican state representative, Joe was extremely conservative, and there was almost nothing on which we agreed, but back when he was in the legislature in 1991, he and a Democrat passed an ethics bill. In 2010, I was working on and trying to pass the first ethics bill since Joe's nineteen years earlier, and the two of us teamed up.

We never talked about any issues other than ethics and campaign reform, and Joe was one of my guys on the inside working the Republican caucus for me.

A few days before the session ended, I stepped out of the chamber into the hallway to strategize with Joe. We talked for a minute before my legislative assistant came to remind me of a speaking engagement I had downstairs in the capitol rotunda. Smiling at the irony, I told my friend from the far religious right, "Joe, I gotta go give a speech to a gay rights rally downstairs. We'll have to pick this up later."

Joe got a big smile on his face and said, "Jason, you just keep doing your thing and I'll keep doing mine and we'll get this bill passed."

And we did. The bill passed in the last hour of the last day of the legislative session.

The other well-known lobbyist for the far religious right was a guy named Kerry Messer. Kerry, unlike Joe, was always trying to convince me we weren't really that far apart on the issues, which was probably why I never trusted him. He sat and talked with me often, but I always felt like I was meeting Kerry's official representative to the outside world instead of Kerry himself.

He was so eager to have his positions be accepted by the mainstream that he would couch them in ways I found dishonest. The last time we spoke was in 2012 when he testified before the judiciary committee and I had the chance to question him.

Kerry was speaking against the Missouri Nondiscrimination Act, a bill I had cosponsored for several years. Better known as MONA, it was a simple proposal to make it illegal to discriminate against LGBT Missourians. In 2012, for the first time, it looked like it might actually pass, so Kerry was trying to kill it without looking too bigoted, which was why he testified that he accepted the fact this was a civil rights issue, but now wasn't "the right time, because Missouri just isn't ready for this yet, even if it is the right thing to do."

My "friendship" with Kerry ended when I said this: "Mr. Messer, thank you for acknowledging this as a civil rights issue. Please name for me a single instance in American history when our country moved too quickly on civil rights."

He could not.

I'm sure Joe Ortwerth and Kerry Messer feel the same way about gay rights, but at least Joe had the courtesy not to try to convince me otherwise.

On the bullshit range, everyone is a safety officer.

On an army marksmanship range, the soldier in charge sits in a tower and uses a loudspeaker to give commands such as "Lock and load your weapon," "Prepare to fire," "Begin firing," "Cease fire," and "Move your selector switch to safe."

Only the soldier in the tower can tell you to start firing. Assistant range officers, who are positioned every two or three firing positions, carry large paddles painted white on one side and red on the other. They use these to signal to the soldier in the tower when they're ready to fire (white) or not ready to fire (red).

But one thing that's made very clear on a firing range

is that "everyone is a safety officer." Any trainer or trainee is empowered to give the order to shut down the range at any moment by repeatedly yelling, "Cease fire! Cease fire! Cease fire!" and waving a hand in front of their face like a windshield wiper in a heavy downpour.

The idea is that everyone, whether they're running the training or just being trained, is responsible for the safety of everyone else.

I often wish we treated lying this way in politics. Whether you're in charge or not, whether it's your business or not, if you know someone is lying and you don't exercise your duty as a safety officer, you should be held accountable whether you're in the tower or the foxhole.

Checking the box: It's like lying but with more words.

"Checking the box" is a commonly used term in the army for someone who technically completes a task but in the most minimal, least valuable way possible, doing just enough to check the box next to that task on a to-do list.

It's more than frowned upon in the army, because the act of "checking the box" can be dangerous. If you pretended to conduct preventative checks and maintenance on a vehicle and it wound up breaking down during a convoy through a combat zone, your check mark put lives at risk.

When politicians check the box, they put the task aside

and act as though the problem is solved when it's not, which—just like in the army—can be worse than doing nothing at all.

I was on the budget committee when the Republicans proposed a faux package of recovery funding after one of the most devastating events in my state's history, the Joplin tornado. The "recovery package" was an unconstitutional bill pretending to spend nonexistent money and con people into believing the state legislature had done something for Joplin.

Worried it would make the prospect of actual relief less likely, I opposed it. Joplin had been through enough. It didn't need phony box-checking dressed up as "relief." Privately, legislators in both parties told me I was right about the bill, but none of them dared say so publicly.

It was well known that I was considering a run for secretary of state if Robin Carnahan chose not to seek reelection, so when I cast the lone no vote in committee, Republicans celebrated. Some openly taunted: "That was a short campaign!"

The vote did come up in both my statewide campaigns, but it lacked the potency they'd hoped for. First of all, who would believe a progressive Democrat was unwilling to spend money on tornado relief? Heck, how many conservative Republicans in southwest Missouri thought a Democrat like me had ever seen *any* government expenditure he didn't immediately fall in love with?

In the end, I think most Joplin voters respected me when

I stood by the vote as an effort to prevent Republicans from hanging a "Mission Accomplished" banner in Joplin.

———

When it comes to keeping it real, it's hard to think of a politician who's done it better than Stephen Webber, a marine who served two tours in Iraq, including one leading a squad in Fallujah. Stephen and I were both elected to the State House in 2008 and became fast friends. Our "bromance" earned several monikers over the years, from "the dynamic duo" to "the military twins."

Our desks were next to each other on the floor of the House; and in 2012, Stephen was balancing law school with his service in the state legislature, so during long debates over meaningless bills everyone knew would pass, he would sometimes pull out a textbook and try to sneak in a few minutes of studying.

During a parade of noncontroversial bills naming stretches of highway and declaring special days of awareness for various causes, he was alternating between studying and shooting the breeze with me.

Meanwhile, a Republican legislator was introducing a bill to designate March 26 as Missouri Iraq and Afghanistan Veterans Day. With a speech about the importance of "acknowledging these brave young men and women," this legislator talked about how honored he was to "be able to do this for them."

At least a dozen other members were standing behind microphones waiting to be called on so they, too, could take credit for this monumental achievement in political box-checking. Stephen was trying, and failing, to ignore it.

"Man, this is ridiculous," he said to me, then set down his textbook, angrily leaped out of his chair, and walked to a microphone. Seeing a genuine Iraq veteran standing to speak, the Speaker skipped everyone else and went straight to recognizing Stephen.

"Mr. Speaker," Stephen said, "I just want to make sure we're all clear on what this is."

He described real veterans' legislation he had filed, which had yet to receive so much as a hearing—bills to provide mental health care, ease the transition from the military to college, and strengthen employment opportunities for vets.

"My friends don't need a day," he said. "My friends need access to counseling. They need college degrees. They need job opportunities, Mr. Speaker, and as a veteran myself, I'm so dang tired of meaningless political gestures by politicians who care more about putting pictures of us on their campaign websites than they do about actually doing anything for us. I'm sure this bill will pass, but I wanted to make sure none of you were under the impression you actually did anything for veterans today, because like most every other day, you did absolutely nothing."

When he concluded, you could feel shame hanging in the air, and everyone previously standing at a microphone waiting to speak had sat down. Stephen, who had no patience for political box-checking, went back to studying.

Have the courage to be more than a walking, talking yellow ribbon car magnet.

Do you remember those yellow ribbon car magnets that used to be popular—the ones that said "Support Our Troops"? Those were everywhere after 9/11, but to my knowledge, very few of those magnet makers sent the proceeds to a charitable cause, so if all you did after 9/11 was put a magnet on your car, I hate to break it to you, but you were zero help to the country.

Politicians who constantly invoke troops or veterans without ever doing anything for either are basically yellow ribbon car magnets personified.

The Veterans Videos program was a state-funded effort to record and preserve interviews with aging Missouri veterans. Giving Missouri families these permanent memories of their loved ones was a worthy pursuit, but when I started asking questions about the details, something smelled.

Each video cost taxpayers $1,400 to shoot, and the company that produced them—"Patriot Productions"— had only one customer: the state of Missouri. Funded through the lieutenant governor's office, the contract had never been put out for a bid.

Patriot Productions spent some of the money it earned from this no-bid contract on a lobbyist whose sole responsibility could only have been convincing Patriot Productions' lone customer to remain a customer. I also discovered the company had made contributions to the campaigns of two politicians: the lieutenant governor who requested funds for Patriot Productions and the budget chairman who oversaw their appropriation.

When I raised a stink about this, the people involved warned me not to make an enemy of Missouri veterans. A colleague publicly accused me of "kicking dirt in the face of our state's vets." Several unsuccessful amendments and one front-page article in the *St. Louis Post-Dispatch* later, the Veterans Video project was cut from the budget.

The program still exists today, but it's known as the Missouri Veterans History Project. Volunteers at the University of Missouri's journalism school produce the videos, and all the expenses are covered by individual donations instead of tax dollars.*

It's common for politicians to invoke the troops when trying to shout down opposition. In the mid-2000s, it was trendy to say that anyone who opposed the war or any of President Bush's decisions regarding the war didn't support the troops. People would say things such as "When

---

* All thanks to state senator Jill Schupp, the very same friend who let me stay rent-free in her spare bedroom many nights.

the troops hear this kind of rhetoric, it's terrible for their morale."

I heard that stuff a lot before I deployed, and then while I was overseas, I realized that we were usually too busy doing important jobs to pay attention to politics—or at least to pay the level of attention necessary for politics to affect our morale. War is a round-the-clock job, and we didn't want to use what little spare mental energy we had on political battles back home.

In my unit, we passed around pop culture magazines like *People* and *Entertainment Weekly* because trivial celebrity gossip asked nothing of us while offering a piece of home.

Once, during an intelligence briefing, Colonel McCracken learned that a group of Imams was speaking out against the broadcasting of Western music in Kabul.

"Well, maybe the Imams think Shakira's hips do, in fact, lie," he deadpanned.

So even the boss was reading the pop culture mags.

Of course, troops and vets aren't alone in getting used by disingenuous politicians intent on playing to a crowd,* but

----

* I've seen a member of Congress with an F rating from the NAACP stand in front of an African American audience, invoke the phrase "Black Lives Matter," and then do a radio interview the next day blaming Ferguson activists for the murder of a New York City police officer.

thanks to the invention of the camera phone, pandering is getting tougher for politicians—one of the upsides to our social media age—because keeping it real is becoming more important than sounding like a talking car magnet.

Once you can fake normal, you've really made it.*

One of the highest compliments you can receive as a politician is to be labeled "a normal person."

When people say, "You really seem comfortable in your own skin," I'm reminded how incredibly low the bar actually is in politics, because I've never heard anyone say, "You know what I love about my accountant? He's just a regular guy."

There's a fancy political word for this: authenticity. When pundits see it in the wild, they try to dissect it, study it, and then explain it. They'll talk about the way you dress, where you're from, and how you speak, but they often miss the point, because the only way for a politician to be authentic is to tell the truth.

You've probably heard someone who personally knows an inauthentic-seeming candidate say some version of, "Those of us who know [him/her] know how [funny/sincere/laid-back] [he/she] is in person."

---

* How have we still not invented a universal sarcasm font?

I've personally known candidates I really liked and considered friends who totally whiffed at connecting with a larger audience. It's frustrating to watch and must be twice as frustrating for them to experience. Sometimes it really is just a matter of their not "feeling comfortable in their own skin" and assuming they have to sound a certain way when they present themselves. I can see how people might think there's a language or a way of doing things that's particular to politics, but there's not.

I remember the moment I learned the political power of keeping it real.

As I've mentioned, I knocked on twenty thousand doors during my first campaign. Luckily, I learned about honesty at one of the very early ones. I was a little nervous as I approached the house and rang the bell, because it looked like someone might actually be home. When I heard the sound of footsteps coming down stairs, I felt a shot of nerves.

A man in his early forties came to the door in bare feet, shorts, and a white T-shirt. He was immediately friendly and listened with interest to my spiel about having come back from Afghanistan earlier that year and wanting to be his state representative because I'd seen what it was like when decisions in government were made solely on politics and not on what's right. As I spoke, he examined the flyer I'd handed him.

"Is there a policy issue that's particularly important to

you?" I asked. He thought about it, then picked one and asked me my view. I no longer remember the issue he chose, but I do remember the look on his face as I gave my answer. It was pretty clear he didn't agree with what I'd said, and when I'd finished talking, he told me as much.

I was brand-new to politicianing, so I did what I'd seen the pros on TV do. I started trying to "spin" my position to make it seem more like his. That only made things worse, because now he had more questions, and our back-and-forth was beginning to feel vaguely like an argument.

This was one of the first meaningful interactions I'd ever had with a voter in my role as a candidate and it wasn't going well, so I started to panic a little. Unhelpful thoughts arose in my mind, like, *I'm terrible at this* and *Should I even be running for office?*

Out of frustration and desperation, I blurted out, "Well, I guess we don't agree on this, but I'm just trying to do what I think is best."

I thanked him for his time, shook his hand, and turned to walk toward the next house when I heard him say, "Yeah, that's fair. OK, I'll vote for you." He gestured toward his front yard, and added, "And you can put a sign out there if you want."

Wait, what?!

Lightbulb moment!

Politics wasn't about correctly answering test questions for voters; it was about demonstrating that you cared enough to say what you believed. He wasn't judging my answer; he was judging my character, and he was doing it in a flash. One conversation on his porch was enough. He wasn't going to go to my website and read every single policy position. Heck, he wasn't even going to read the other side of my flyer.

From that moment on, I was addicted to holding an honest conversation with the electorate—whether in person or over the airwaves.

Be a person. Not a pretzel.

Over the years, I've watched my fellow politicians—friends of mine—twist into pretzels trying to navigate the political terrain, and it always looks so damn stressful. How do they remember why they took a position in the past, and how do they answer questions about it now?

My way is easier and less stressful. When someone asks me why I said something a few years ago, all I have to ask myself is why I would have thought that then. If I did the political pretzel routine, I'd also have to ask myself what was going on politically then and why I might have taken that position. That's too much to remember.

It's like your mother told you when you were ten years old: if you always tell the truth, you only have to remember what happened.

Voters so seldom hear the honest truth that it's disarming

(and effective) when they do. If value is highest where scarcity meets demand, truth is the most valuable commodity in politics.

Right about now you're thinking, *Well, that sounds nice, but what about all the people who've been successful in politics by employing deception?*

Yes, you can sometimes win that way, but here's something to ponder: How many of the politicians you're thinking of seem to be enjoying life? How many end up doing more than just putting a win on the board?

For most deceptive politicians—good actors doing bad acts—deception is employed for the same reason they entered politics. They see all of it as a means to an end—a way to win one election or get to the immediate next level. But it will eventually catch up to them.

You can sometimes win an election by being inauthentic, but your chances of victory go down each successive time you try.

And here's the most important part: lying might help you win, but it won't do anything to advance what you truly believe, which is supposed to be the whole point of running in the first place. You can get where you're going by pretending to believe something you don't, but you won't win the long-term argument or achieve the change you want to see in the world.

I've batted .750 in campaigns, but if I had the chance to go back in time and sell out my values to bat .1000, I wouldn't even consider it, because I don't define success by winning elections. I define it by changing things for the better.

So it all comes down to just doing what I believe—doing the right thing—every single day. And then getting up tomorrow and doing it again.

If that's your standard of political success, then the truth is your greatest weapon and—though I may sound like a Boy Scout—being a good politician becomes no different than trying to be a good person.

Shalom, y'all.

I'm not one of these people who feels that "political correctness run amok" is an actual problem in America. I see nothing wrong with all of us trying to be decent to one another. When someone says something has offended them, I take them at their word, but I've also noticed in politics that opportunities to feign offense when you don't mean it do present themselves.*

Let me preface what I'm about to say with this: As a straight white male, I'm well aware that I speak from a privileged position and am almost never the target of offensive speech or acts. So what little experience I have with this comes from being the third Jew ever to hold statewide

---

* In sports, they call it "flopping."

office in the history of Missouri, and what I've learned is to stop and ask myself whether I'm truly offended before I act offended.

In 2012, when a political organization in a rural Missouri county invited me to come out to speak to their members about my campaign for secretary of state, the group's leader gave some unsolicited advice to my scheduler.

"Now, I don't want to cast aspersions, but is it true Mr. Kander's not a Christian?"

"That's right," she said. "Jason is Jewish."

"Oh, OK, that's what we had heard, but we thought it might be a rumor. Well, that's OK, but would you please let him know that while that might play well in Kansas City, it's best not to lead with it here?"

When this exchange was first relayed to me, I wondered why I didn't feel offended, and then I realized I was seeing it from that person's point of view. There was a good chance I was the first Jew a lot of these people would ever knowingly meet, and this nice woman organizing the event was only trying to be helpful. Obviously, it was a little odd that she thought I might open my speech talking about my religion, but not when you consider how often other politicians in Missouri began by talking about their Christian faith.

I did the speech and it went fine, but all week I kept jokingly telling my staff I was going to start it with, "Shalom, y'all!" which became the campaign's unofficial motto.

A few months later, I was staying over at the home of a good friend in Parma, Missouri, population six hundred. Parma is in what we call the "bootheel," which is the little piece of southeast Missouri that hangs down into Arkansas and Tennessee. The Mason-Dixon Line runs along Missouri's southern border, and most Missourians identify more as Midwesterners than as Southerners, but from the syrupy drawls to the cotton crops, the bootheel is unmistakably the American South.

So there I was, hanging out and chatting it up in the living room with my buddy, his father-in-law, and a member of my campaign staff. My buddy's father-in-law started to tell a joke, and about a quarter of the way through, it became pretty apparent he was telling a Jewish joke.

I leaned in and half raised a hand to gently interrupt. When he paused, I said, "Sir, I'm sure you won't offend me or anything, but before you finish, I feel like I should tell you that I'm Jewish."

I really didn't expect to be offended. I just didn't want him to feel uncomfortable if he found out after telling the joke. He laughed the kind of laugh you laugh when you think someone is pulling your leg, and finished the joke, which was pretty mild and didn't bother me.

My buddy then said to his father-in-law, "He's not kidding, you know. He really is Jewish."

"Really? Jeez, I thought you were kidding. Hope you're not mad at me."

I assured him I wasn't, but I could feel the awkwardness in the room, so I decided to make him feel better by inviting him to give me a little advice. He had mentioned earlier he was involved as some sort of lay clergy in his church, and I was going to church with a fellow state representative the next morning so that I could meet people. In reality, I had done this numerous times already on the campaign trail and wasn't at all concerned about it;* nonetheless, I laid out a chance for him to be of service: "I'm going to church in Caruthersville tomorrow morning. I'm sure people will ask me what church I go to in Kansas City, but I don't go to church, I go to synagogue. What should I say?"

Old boy thought on this for a moment, shrugged his shoulders, waved his hand in a "no big deal" motion, and said, "Long as you're Christian, ain't nobody gonna have a problem with ya."

My buddy, exasperated, leaned toward him and said, "He's not Christian! He's Jewish, remember?"

"Oh, right. Yeah, jeez, that is different, I guess." He crossed his arms, looked up at the ceiling in thought, and said, "Pssh, a Jew's just another kind of Christian."

That, of course, made no sense, but everyone felt much better.

---

* Not to mention having been the only Jew at a Catholic high school.

"Be nice... until it's time to not be nice."*

In February 2013, just a few weeks after I was sworn in as secretary of state, I flew to DC for my first National Association of Secretaries of State meeting.**

NASS has been around forever, and, historically, it's been a professional association for secretaries of state to exchange best practices about stuff like election administration, business registration, and securities regulation. Until Secretary Kris Kobach of Kansas came along, NASS had never been all that political.

Kris was and is a hard-right, race-baiting opportunist with a frightening superpower: a tone and speaking style that disguise dangerous ideas as helpful commonsense proposals. He is always well mannered, especially when he's lying.

Having shared a border and a media market (Kansas City) with Kris for years, I knew his game, so when he came to NASS bearing a letter he'd written to President Obama, I figured it probably wasn't to congratulate the president on his recent reelection.

During his victory speech on election night in 2012, President Obama had improvised a line about the need

---

* Patrick Swayze in *Road House* (the *Citizen Kane* of movies about Missouri country-western bars).
** Every bit the raging party you'd expect it to be.

to cut down on wait times at polling places, and several Democratic members of Congress had since introduced legislation to address the problem.

Given Kris's passion for treating voters like criminal suspects instead of customers, he'd come to NASS armed with a resolution calling on the federal government to stay out of election administration and leave it to the states.

A tense but unceasingly polite debate ensued among the secretaries of state seated around the large conference room.

I say "polite" because while a few Republicans had reservations about the resolution, the majority of its skeptics were Democrats, and all of its proponents were newly elected Tea Party Republicans who worshipped Kris Kobach. Given the collegial and nonpartisan history of the organization, everyone was gingerly stepping around the subject.

When someone suggested the resolution might make NASS appear to be taking a partisan position, Kris feigned shock at such a preposterous idea. "There's nothing partisan about a bunch of state election officials telling the federal government to keep out of our elections," he said.

As the new guy, I had hardly spoken up yet, and since I was from Missouri, half the people in the room assumed I was a Republican anyway. Not wanting to make a scene on day one, I had been reserved so far, but that was about to come to an end.

"Secretary Kobach, of course it's partisan," I said. "You're obviously trying to use NASS for your own partisan agenda."*

An awkward and uncomfortable vibe invaded the room. A few secretaries cleared their throats and shifted in their seats.

"Oh, c'mon now," he said in a tone meant to suggest he was disappointed in me. "I'm frankly offended by that, Jason." He shook his head disapprovingly and everything. Damn, he was scary good. I wouldn't have been surprised if he'd actually said, "Tsk-tsk-tsk," and wagged his finger at me.

"Everyone is talking around it," I said, "but we should acknowledge what we're really talking about here. Hell yes, it's partisan, because one party wants to keep the federal government out of our elections and the other party wants to let black people vote."

Actual gasps.

Alison Lundergan Grimes, Kentucky's secretary of state, leaned over to me and whispered, "Kander, you and I are gonna be friends."**

Over the next two days, the conference devolved into

---

* Voter suppression is a big part of the Republican Party's political strategy, and Kris Kobach is their vote suppressor in chief. More on this in Lesson Number Nine (including the story of how and why I founded Let America Vote), but basically Kris is the unofficial leader of an unofficial group, which, I assume, calls itself Don't Let America Vote.
** Accurate prediction on her part.

a skirmish over Kris's resolution, and at one point it got so crazy that I—a dude who had been there all of five minutes—distributed a proposed change to NASS's decades-old bylaws, which would have required any resolution with partisan implications to gain a supermajority of votes in order to pass.

On the final day of the conference, after a fierce debate, Kris's voter suppression resolution failed in a close vote, and I headed home to Missouri having failed to make any new friends among the Tea Party contingent.

On the important stuff—like standing up for democracy—remember to keep it real. The more uncomfortable it makes those around you, the more likely it is you're speaking the truth.

Politics can be completely absurd. Deal with it.

"Hooah" is an army term that can mean anything except "no."

In a given day, the average soldier uses several hooahs—probably with a slightly different meaning each time—to communicate agreement, understanding, excitement, or just to say something is good. The word itself is a ubiquitous part of army life and culture.

When I was training officer candidates at Fort Mc-Clellan, Alabama, in 2009, I sensed poor cohesion and low morale among the platoon I was training, so I found an empty cardboard box that once held meals ready to eat, presented it to the platoon, and announced, "This box is full of hooah! It shall henceforth be known as the 'box of hooah.'"

A small acknowledgment of absurdity gave the platoon license to adopt an attitude of faux seriousness toward the box and introduce a little fun into their training. Never breaking character from this routine, the box was treated as though it were a vital piece of military equipment imbued with immense power. When another platoon's trainer asked one of my officer candidates what was up with this weird cardboard box stuff, the OC responded with a straight face, "Sir, this is the box of hooah. It can heal wounds, sir! Unconfirmed reports indicate it might also have the capacity to move oceans, sir!"

Everywhere the platoon went, the box of hooah went, too, precipitating the creation of some hilariously intricate procedures supposedly outlined in an army manual on box of hooah maintenance. Out in the field, it was wrapped in plastic and covered in ponchos during wet weather. In the barracks, after lights-out, an officer candidate guarded it while the platoon slept. At every company formation, our platoon sergeant would face his troops and—with great seriousness and at full volume—order the platoon to "Preeeezent... box!" at which point forty officer candidates would sing "hoooooooooooah" as the box was held aloft like Simba in *The Lion King*.

One of my fellow trainers criticized me for permitting all this nonsense, referring to me as "Captain Camp Counselor" and calling my motivational technique "Mickey Mouse shit."

Our commander, however, saw nothing wrong, and he even seemed to enjoy these antics.

As a training officer, I was not all fun and games. I

handed out plenty of push-ups, yelled until I lost my voice, and hardly ever smiled, because that's how you carry yourself when you're a platoon trainer responsible for maintaining the "stressful and demanding environment of OCS."

The rules of OCS are essential to the training process, because without preposterously detailed protocols, officer candidates might never learn their capacity to maintain calm under pressure. By the same token, however, OCS is necessarily tedious and insane. By doing more than just shouting and sneering, I bought credibility in the eyes of my platoon when I subtly acknowledged the lunacy surrounding all of us. When my phase of training at Fort McClellan OCS ended, my officer candidates tore off a piece of the box, signed it, and sent me home with it.

As you can no doubt tell from what you've read so far in this book, I've never considered a touch of levity to automatically indicate a deficit of seriousness—as long as I get the timing right and I don't go overboard with the dosage. Constantly pointing out absurdity smacks of cynicism, while denying its existence looks like cluelessness, so I've always tried to live somewhere between the two.

Pretending to be "above the game" never works in life or in politics, which is why politicians who deny being politicians seem so phony. Since leaving office and starting Let America Vote, reporters have asked me if I still consider myself a politician, and even though most people in my line of work would jump at the chance to shed the politician label, I never do.

I'm trying to change the world for the better, my chosen method for doing so is politics, and I've personally run for office four times and probably will again, so yes, of course I'm a politician.

Is it less dignified to be referred to as a politician? Probably. I won't compromise my integrity to get ahead, but I'll gladly cash in my dignity for a good cause.

It doesn't get more ridiculous than the money chase.

Just before noon on Monday, January 14, 2013, I was sworn in as Missouri's thirty-ninth secretary of state. No real work got done that first day, unless you count a parade, a ceremony, and a big fancy ball in the capitol. My first full day on the job was Tuesday the fifteenth.

After a busy morning and lunch hour, I sat down at my new desk to read and sign a tall stack of documents already awaiting my approval and signature. Before I could get started, Phyllis, my new assistant, came through the door with a question.

"Do you know a James Dowd?"

"Jim Dowd? Sure do!" I said. I was in the kind of mood where everything ended in an exclamation point and a smile.

The Dowds, for several generations, have been a prolific St. Louis Democratic family with so many branches that it seemed I was always meeting new Dowds.

"Apparently he's downstairs at reception and just stopped by to congratulate you," she said. "Should I just have them say you're busy?"

"Jim is *here*? I can take a moment to say hi; let's bring him upstairs!"

So on my first day as a statewide elected official, I stopped what I was doing to take an impromptu meeting with a guy I was pretty sure had written a check to my campaign.

A few minutes later, Phyllis ushered in an elderly gentleman who looked pretty surprised to be there. I bet I looked just as surprised, because this wasn't Jim Dowd from St. Louis. "Hi, Mr. Secretary, I'm James Dowd from here in Jefferson City," he said as we shook hands. "I just wanted to send my congratulations, but I'm tickled you'd take the time to visit."

I didn't want to be rude, so I invited James to have a seat. Turned out he was an attorney who had worked in our counsel's office thirty years prior and, in retirement, had made it a habit to stop by and express well wishes at the beginning of each new term.

"But this is my first time getting to do it in person!" he said with a laugh.

I asked if he was related to the St. Louis Dowds and he said he wasn't, but that he got that question anytime he met a politician.

We visited for about fifteen minutes, and I actually really enjoyed hearing about the old days.

As I watched James walk down the hall to leave, I

thought about the craziness of politics and the obvious influence of money on politicians. Before even learning how to work the thermostat in my office, I'd taken a pickup meeting with a man I'd never met simply because he had the same name as a supporter.

Money influences EVERYONE in politics, without exception.

I wish this weren't true, but it is, and it's why the system is so badly in need of change. The question of money's influence on our politics isn't one of guilt or innocence—it's a question of degree—because no one's fully innocent. Not even self-funders or those powered by the grass roots are immune, because a billionaire candidate knows a position stand can cause the opponent's fund-raising to go up or down, and a campaign funded by small-dollar donations knows the well can go dry with just one statement antithetical to the beliefs of its base.

I do my level best to be immune to the influence of political money, but I know I've been guilty of returning phone calls with greater urgency when I'm aware that the person on the other end of the phone wrote a big campaign check.

This is especially true at the beginning of a political career, because when your list of supporters is small, you

can't help but remember who did what, and it's human nature to be grateful.*

I know I'm in politics for the right reasons, and I'm supremely confident I've never given special treatment to a donor. And yet—no matter how hard I may try—I'll never fully flush from my brain the knowledge of who gave big.

It's why we need to get money out of politics as best we can by, at a minimum, bringing back real contribution limits and, ideally, moving to a publicly financed campaign system. Given that I've been reasonably successful at raising political money, many have called me a hypocrite for holding this position, but there's nothing hypocritical about playing within the rules of the game while simultaneously working to change those rules.

For instance, I believe the American League's designated hitter rule has been bad for baseball, but I don't want my Kansas City Royals benching their designated hitter and handing a bat to the pitcher in the name of ideological purity.

There's no way this is making our democracy better.

The total spent by campaigns and outside groups from both sides of my 2016 US Senate race was $75 million,

---

* And it's "politician nature" to ask for more.

making it—by a long shot—the most expensive race in state history.

Sometimes it felt like all I did was raise money. If I wasn't in the "call room" asking people for money over the phone, I was probably in a meeting or a fund-raising event, asking in person. When traveling between in-person asks, I was in the backseat of the car with a binder of donor call sheets on my lap and a phone to my ear.

I always looked forward to any non-fund-raising event on the calendar. Rallies and speeches energized me, but as soon as we got back on the road, I was back on the phone. I did so much call time inside a moving vehicle that I would get carsick from looking down, so I began wearing motion sickness bracelets.

Given the money required to run, a highly competitive Senate race is essentially a national campaign, because the amount a candidate can raise inside their state is only about half of what's called for in the campaign budget. So for twenty-one months I averaged at least three nights per week raising money *outside* Missouri.

I must have made twenty different trips just to New York City alone.

You'd probably assume a Missouri Democrat running for Senate would never get to know the other Democratic Senate candidates around the country, but you'd be wrong. We did events together all over America.

On several occasions, I bumped into fellow candidates

on the street in places like Chicago, Los Angeles, and New York. Each time, we were in states none of us called home.

Sometimes I'd show up at a restaurant for a meeting with a prospective donor just as they wrapped up an appointment with a candidate from another state. I'd say, "Boy, this campaign finance system sure is working great, huh?"*

Like it was political speed dating, I'd spend thirty minutes saying a lot of the same stuff I'd said in the last meeting, and then I'd do it again and again. It became so repetitive that I was constantly afraid I might forget the name of the person across the table.

Actually, scratch that. There were plenty of times when I did forget the person's name, so what I feared was one of them calling me on it—just looking me dead in the eye and saying, "Quick. Who am I?"

Fifteen minutes into a donor meeting in Denver, my nightmare became my reality when the man across the table asked me, "Have you ever met John Smith?"

Uh-oh.

I thought *this* guy was John Smith!

This is it, I thought. *He's on to me.*

Lacking a better plan, I bit the bullet. "Aren't...you John Smith?"

He looked at me like he thought that was a pretty dumb

---

* Not once did that line get a laugh.

thing to say. "Of course," he replied. "I'm talking about a different John Smith."

I exhaled and laughed really hard. John, lacking the context going on inside my brain, laughed politely.

A few minutes later, John walked us out, handed over a check, and promised to put us in touch with the other John Smith. As we walked to our next meeting, I laughed so hard my staffer thought I had gone insane.

With my little black rolling suitcase struggling to navigate the cobblestone streets of downtown Denver, I felt as though the campaign had finally reached peak absurdity.

That little suitcase, by the way, was the perfect metaphor for this foolishness, and wheeling it around the entire country was a never-ending source of amusement to me. The schedule rarely had me in one place for more than a night—we'd schedule meetings and events up until the last moment and I'd hustle to the airport, sprint to TSA, and barely make my flight. As a result, I always had to keep my bags with me; so there I was, wearing a suit and pulling that suitcase behind me into meetings and fund-raisers.*

Every time the Republicans would hit me for fundraising out of state, I wanted to respond, "It's your system! You made this! Don't blame me for playing by your own dumb rules."

---

* I was always tempted to begin appointments by putting the suitcase up on the desk and saying, "Just wait until you see this vacuum in action!"

Abe always talked me out of responding that way.*

Early in the campaign, we did a young-professionals fund-raiser in DC. It was a low-dollar event a bunch of my longtime friends who lived in the area could afford to attend, so the guests were a mix of my college, law school, and army pals.

That morning, I'd woken up feeling ill. I was having trouble keeping food down, lacked energy, and dragged myself through a day on the phone and attending meetings. I called Claire McCaskill to ask her whether she thought I should cancel the fund-raiser. "Jason, my schedule's open tonight," she said. "I'll go, I'll give the speech on your behalf, and you can just show up and introduce me."

So the event starts and—even though I'm woozy and not at my best—I get up to introduce Claire. With my head as foggy as it was, I hadn't noticed the Republican trackers standing above me on a balcony taking video, and I began by saying how excited I was "to see so many of my friends in one place" and that it felt "like a wedding."

By the time I got home to Kansas City the next morning, a clip of "so-called Washington outsider Jason Kander" hobnobbing with his close friends in Washington was buzzing around social media.

The Republicans—desperate to tarnish my "fresh-faced

---

* As usual, he was right.

image"*—went to great lengths to smear me as a money-grubbing Washington insider, even making some poor GOP intern dress up in a panda costume and follow me around whenever I was in DC.**

For each Washington fund-raiser, we had to devise a panda plan of ingress and egress to get me in and out of buildings without allowing the tracker to get footage of the panda and me in the same frame.

I actually got a kick out of this little game. On one occasion, after sneaking in a back entrance, a couple of dozen supporters and I watched through the front windows of a restaurant as a passing kindergarten class smothered the panda in hugs.

To the intern in the panda suit's credit, he posed for pictures with all the kids and it was kind of adorable.

If you think this nutty fund-raising system makes sense, you're already out of touch.

Now that I'm shoulders-deep into this screed about our broken campaign finance system, I'll clarify that I'm not

---

* They literally ran an attack ad where my face morphed into those of Nancy Pelosi and Bernie Sanders while a scary voice warned, "Jason Kander. He's no fresh face."

** Kander rhymes with pander, which sounds a little like panda, thus the ads where "Jason Kander the Pandering Panda" danced while money fell from the sky.

asking you to feel sorry for me, because at least 90 percent of this "work" is preferable to sitting at a desk writing a response to a summary judgment motion. The two points I do wish to communicate are: (1) This is a really dumb way to run a democracy; and (2) It's a grind, and people don't do it just for fun.

I actually think that second point is an important one, and too few pundits and reporters get it. Early in the campaign, a well-known pundit speculated about why I'd entered the race, positing I knew it was unwinnable but that my real goal was increased name recognition just in case Senator McCaskill chose not to run for reelection and I was the Democratic nominee in 2018.

As I imagined the idea of going through all of this only to afford myself the privilege of turning around and doing it again, I laughed out loud, which probably looked maniacal to the people around me in the gate area. It was early morning and I—still wearing a suit—had just woken up from a nap on an airport floor.

Believe it or not, I didn't hate fund-raising. I figured anyone who could give a couple thousand dollars over the phone to someone they had never heard of until five minutes earlier had probably done some interesting stuff in their life. And I got to talk to them about it.

I'd often start these conversations with something like, "Now, I'm obviously going to ask you for money in a minute, but before I do, I'm a huge space nerd, so can we talk about your old job at NASA first?"

Whenever I'd come to a call sheet for the owner or part owner of a sports franchise, someone on staff would plead with me not to give them unsolicited advice.*

If nothing stood out in their bio, I'd open with a question so out of left field they'd feel compelled to answer it. Next thing they knew, they were in a conversation with me about the most random stuff.

"Howdy. I'm Jason Kander. Ever been to Missouri?"

"Hey there, you're the victim of a good old-fashioned fund-raising call. How many politicians have already called you today, and, if I'm not the first, do you have any money left?"

By the end of the campaign, believe it or not, I had made real friends in every part of the country.

But at least once every day while on the road, I'd say out loud to someone that spending 96 percent of my time with people for whom America had worked out perfectly probably wasn't preparing me to be a better senator. And I was the Democratic candidate, so at least most of those people wanted to talk about what could be done for the people who couldn't afford to get on my out-of-state travel schedule.

I suspect Republican candidates don't find themselves discussing the working and middle class quite so often in these fund-raising meetings, but I can't say for sure.

---

* If Baltimore Orioles owner Peter Angelos is reading this, I stand by everything I said about David Lough's potential. And also, sir, I'm sorry if I offended you with my joke about the 2014 American League Championship Series (#BuryMeARoyal).

Sometimes the frustration with the whole system would get the best of me. I'd wheel my little suitcase up to somebody's house, sit down in their living room, and they'd ask me some innocent icebreaker question like, "So, how ya doin'?" and I'd reply with something like, "Can we talk about how ridiculous it is that I'm here right now?" When they got over the shock, we'd end up having a refreshing conversation and I'd usually earn their support.

Here's my point: there's no way this system is making us better as a country, because the money chase holds no actual societal value and only accelerates the process by which a politician loses touch with the experience of the people that politician is supposed to represent.

Before I ran for the Senate, I knew politicians could often be out of touch, but I never understood how some in Washington became so seemingly disconnected from what regular people were going through. Now that I've run for the Senate, I realize it's largely due to the fund-raising schedule.

What if we designed a system where every politician in America had more conversations with regular people than with the kind of people regular people almost never meet? It would make an enormous difference.

The years I've spent raising political money have taught me to laugh at the strangest parts by reminding myself there's nothing normal about running the money gauntlet. Politicians who lose sight of that cease to be the people voters liked in the first place.

And since we're on the subject of big problems in need

of attention, if fund-raising is the most nonsensical feature of our democracy, redistricting is a close second.

The party of green dots must be stopped.

Right now, the biggest problem in national politics is that we have so many people in Washington of whom it can truthfully be said that the toughest thing they've ever voluntarily been through in their lives is the campaign that got them there in the first place. If landing your job was the hardest experience of your life, you probably think losing that job would be the worst thing that could happen to you, and, therefore, you're willing to do anything to keep it.

Never underestimate an election winner's tendency to draw inspiration from the fairness of the system that produced their victory. That's why people who ran on a platform of systemic change sometimes lose interest in reform.

Every ten years, after the census, states redraw their congressional and state legislative districts. Every state does it differently, but few do it fairly.

Most allow the state legislature to draw congressional districts, which is dumb because the majority party totally dominates and creates transparently partisan boundaries.

States like South Dakota and Michigan take it a step further. Their process is a special kind of corrupt double down, because in those states the state legislature also draws their *own* district maps. That's dumb upon dumb—or corrupt upon corrupt—and it's no coincidence that these are the two most gerrymandered states in America.

In Missouri, the state legislature draws the congressional maps, but a bipartisan panel of political operatives and pals appointed by elected officials gets together to draw the districts of state legislators. Theoretically, this takes the elected legislators—and therefore the partisan bias—out of the process. But that's just a facade because, as you could tell from an earlier story I shared with you, legislators are constantly updated on the maps as they're developed.

Though not technically part of the redistricting process, incumbent members know what's going on and work the panel to render their reelections as safe as possible. Because this involves incumbents of both parties, it makes Democratic districts safely blue and Republican districts safely red.

Yes, the majority party gains a greater advantage in rigging the game for their side, but the incumbent members of the minority party are too often coconspirators preserving their own seats.

Even before I was a statewide candidate, I mostly ignored the gossip about how my district would be affected. I figured no matter what district they drew on the map, I would just go out and meet the voters and do my best to win. Every time someone referred to my district as "the Kander district," I pushed back that it belonged to the voters, not to me.

In Missouri, term limits prohibit a representative from

serving more than eight years, and the map was going to last ten years. How could the district belong to me when I couldn't even represent it for the full life of its existence?

The green dots were the most offensive part of the process. In the mapping technology used by the redistricting commission, every representative's residence was marked by a green dot, and some representatives lived within blocks of each other, meaning two green dots would be within centimeters of each other on the map. The commission would go to great lengths to ensure that no two incumbents were drawn into the same district, because it was sacrosanct that forcing two incumbents to run against each other in a primary was to be avoided at all costs. From coast to coast and border to border, you'd be surprised how many squiggly lines are created to make sure we never have to lose any of our nation's most precious asset: politicians.*

A decade of representative democracy is determined by the addresses of a few citizens, and everyone acts like this is normal!

As is the case with campaign finance laws, candidates run for office saying the redistricting system is in need of change. But too often the winners wind up inspired into inaction. They won! The people's voice was heard!

Then they switch parties, but not from Democrat to Republican or vice versa. They join the Party of Green Dots.

---

* Dear opposition researcher assigned to my file by the Republican National Committee: that was sarcasm.

Unified control by the Party of Green Dots prevents us from ending gerrymandering, but it also prevents us from implementing worthy reforms like jungle primaries or ranked choice voting.*

We don't allow criminal defendants to serve on their own juries, so we shouldn't allow politicians to draw their own districts. It's dumb, and we should quit doing it.

In fact, redistricting should be more like the actual jury system. Bring in a random group of citizens, don't ask their political party, have a judge instruct them on the importance of the civic duty they're about to perform, give them mapping technology with the green dots turned off, and sequester them for a week.

They'll emerge with a fair map hated by elected officials in both parties—which is how we'll know they nailed it.

Successfully navigating a shamefully broken system should only deepen your obligation to repair it.

There are two types of people who successfully ascend the ladders of life: those who pull up the ladder behind them and those who spend their time looking for more ladders to lower.

When real-estate developers put Kansas City together,

---

* Reforms that give every vote equal impact even in districts heavily weighted to one party.

they created housing contracts prohibiting African Americans and Jews from buying homes in certain neighborhoods, but in 1948, the US Supreme Court ruled these "racially restrictive covenants" unconstitutional. Over the decade-plus that followed, Jewish families like the Kanders slowly started moving into these sections of town, but African American families were far less welcomed. In fact, selling a house to a black family was referred to as "breaking the block."

Around 1960, my grandfather Ed Kander (whom we call "Pop"), my grandmother, my dad, and my aunt and uncle moved into one of these neighborhoods. Shortly thereafter, Pop was more or less drafted into becoming president of the neighborhood association, which his new neighbors assured him wasn't much work.

Here's how Pop described it: "The biggest responsibility was that the neighborhood association president was also the coach of the baseball team, which was fine by me. The team was decent and I was going to the games anyway because your dad and your uncle both played. We didn't have a kid who could play shortstop, so hunting for a shortstop was the toughest part of being neighborhood association president."

But later that summer one of the families down the street sold their home to a shady out-of-towner who opened a boardinghouse, which was basically just an unlicensed hotel. Everyone was up in arms over the idea of all these strangers coming and going at all hours to a house in the middle of their peaceful residential neighborhood, so they called upon President Pop to take legal action.

Pop wasn't a lawyer, but the law was clearly on his side, so he was able to go to court and navigate the process. Weeks later, as the case was about to be heard by a judge, the attorney for the boardinghouse owners found Pop outside the courtroom and issued a threat: "If this case goes forward, you'll probably win, but you should know that my client has already identified a black family interested in moving into your neighborhood. If you don't drop your case right now, my client is breaking your block."

Even though he knew not everyone in the neighborhood would want him to ignore the threat and press forward, Pop didn't skip a beat. He smiled at the lawyer and said, "That's great! We'd love to have them."

Then Pop very earnestly asked, "Do you happen to know if this new family has a kid who can play shortstop?"

If you find yourself elected to office, I hope you'll never give in to the temptation to believe your victory vindicates the process, because it doesn't. On the contrary, you're probably the exception, and now you have an even greater responsibility to use your position to lower more ladders and widen the path for those coming up behind you.

If at any point you feel this connection with reality slipping away, get an empty box, fill it with hooah, and remember not to take yourself too seriously.

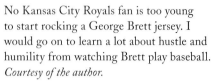

No Kansas City Royals fan is too young to start rocking a George Brett jersey. I would go on to learn a lot about hustle and humility from watching Brett play baseball. *Courtesy of the author.*

My mom, Janet Kander, raised her boys to believe they were unstoppable. *Courtesy of the author.*

My younger brother Jeff and I couldn't take on bears like this one without some backup. In the early nineties, our mom and dad took in boys from our neighborhood whose families were struggling. Jeff and I refer to them as our "unofficial foster brothers." *Courtesy of the author.*

My dad—who was also my coach—used baseball to teach me about life and what kind of man he wanted me to be. *Courtesy of the author.*

Diana and I have been together since we were seventeen years old. Here we are with my mom and dad at a social function in the summer before we started college. *Courtesy of the author.*

After 9/11, I joined the Army ROTC and enlisted in the Army National Guard. This was taken during a training exercise in 2003. *Courtesy of the author.*

Crammed into a "cattle car" with my squad at Fort Lewis in 2004. Since 9/11, tons of service members—including most of the soldiers in this photo—have done more and had it tougher than I have. I'm still driven by a desire to live up to their examples. *Courtesy of the author.*

Convoy duty in Afghanistan. In training, they told us that when we got overseas we'd have armored Humvees. In reality, I spent nearly all my "outside the wire" time in unarmored civilian Mitsubishi Pajeros like those pictured here. *Courtesy of the author.*

Pulling security during a return trip to Kabul from Jalalabad in December 2006. My job as an intelligence officer was to investigate Afghan government and military officials suspected of corruption, espionage, and narco-trafficking. Doing it right meant getting out there and talking to people.

Abdul Jabar Sabet was the attorney general of Afghanistan and my favorite contact within the Afghan government because he spoke fluent English, was highly placed, and—one frightening encounter aside—had no discernable incentive to help anyone kidnap me. *Courtesy of the author.*

My closest friend over there was my primary translator, Salam. In intelligence school, I was advised not to let my translators find out that I'm Jewish, but when I told Salam, he asked, "Did you think I didn't know that?" *Courtesy of the author.*

When I came home, I was assigned as a platoon trainer for the Army National Guard's Officer Candidate School. *Courtesy of the author.*

In 2008, at the age of 26, I entered a three-way Democratic primary to represent Kansas City in the state legislature. The whole family pitched in. Here I am stuffing envelopes with my mom and dad. *Courtesy of the author.*

Celebrating an improbable landslide victory on election night 2008 with my family. *Courtesy of the author.*

Jews used to be banned from living in Kansas City's Brookside neighborhood. When the law changed, Ed Kander moved into Brookside with his family. Fifty years later, he saw his neighbors elect his grandson to represent them in the state legislature. *Courtesy of Eric Bowers.*

In 2010, I teamed up with Republican state representative Tim Flook (left) to push ethics and campaign reforms. The Speaker of the House was no fan of our work and started referring to me by a vulgar nickname. *Courtesy of Tim Bommell.*

Stephen Webber (left) and I were both elected in 2008. Stephen is a Marine who did two tours in Iraq and took no guff from anyone in the legislature. Quite a pair from the start, we became known as "the dynamic duo." *Courtesy of the* Columbia Daily Tribune */ August Kryger.*

In 2008, I personally knocked on 20,000 doors. After I was elected, I kept right on knocking. In 2010, I was reelected with 70 percent of the vote. *Courtesy of Eric Bowers.*

Knocking again in 2011 with my mentor Sly James during his long shot bid to unseat Kansas City's incumbent mayor. Some people thought I was nuts to endorse a guy nobody had ever heard of, but I believed in Sly. Today, Sly is the best mayor in America. *Courtesy of the author.*

Six million people live in Missouri, so I couldn't knock on every door when I ran for secretary of state. Instead, Abe and I put 90,000 miles on his Ford Escape, getting to every county or town fair in Missouri. *Courtesy of the author.*

I spent a lot of time in the "call room" asking people for money a couple hundred bucks at a time. I stayed in shape by doing pushups whenever I got a yes. The other side had richer donors, but we "worked from the have to."
Courtesy of the author.

Diana and I making get-out-the-vote calls from a Democratic field office in the final days of my secretary of state campaign. We do everything as a team. *Courtesy of the author.*

Around 1:00 am on election night, someone high-fived my dad as he viewed a screen showing us in the lead for the first time. *Courtesy of the author.*

I take a congratulatory call from Missouri governor Jay Nixon just after the race is called in our favor. My campaign manager, Abe Rakov (right), was the architect of our underdog victory on the same day President Obama lost Missouri by almost ten points. *Courtesy of the author.*

Diana looks on as I take the oath of office and become Missouri's thirty-ninth secretary of state. *Courtesy of the author.*

Diana, Missouri attorney general Chris Koster, me, and Jennifer Cullen take a break during the inaugural ball in January 2013. A year and a half earlier, Chris helped persuade me to run for secretary of state by telling me, "Jason, if you're willing to put yourself out there and fail—to be publicly humiliated in front of all your friends and family—that makes you very dangerous to the status quo." *Courtesy of Dustin Allison.*

As secretary of state, I fought for the right of every eligible voter to cast a ballot. Unfortunately, that's a radical idea at the moment. *Courtesy of the author.*

During my 2016 campaign for the US Senate, I made it to each of our state's 114 counties. What I learned above all is that everyone wants their family to be happy, healthy, safe, and nearby. We could do a better job of addressing the nearby part. *Courtesy of the author.*

Vice President Joe Biden (right) campaigned for me multiple times, including at this rally at the Pageant Theater in St. Louis. *Courtesy of Suzy Smith.*

Making Senator Elizabeth Warren laugh during a campaign stop in Kansas City. *Courtesy of Sarah Starnes.*

Taking selfies with supporters during a visit from Senator Cory Booker. *Courtesy of the* St. Louis American/ *Wiley Price.*

Mark Putnam, my media consultant, looks on as we film the ad heard round the world. I am a proud recipient of an F rating from the NRA, and rather than pretend otherwise, we made an argument for gun reform while demonstrating I knew what the heck I was talking about. *Courtesy of the author.*

On the campaign RV with True, comparing hand sizes well past his bedtime. He called our RV "the daddy bus." *Courtesy of Suzy Smith.*

I must have made twenty out-of-state fund-raising trips to New York City alone. Here I am at a fund-raiser in the Big Apple as my great uncle, John Kander, looks on. John is a Broadway composer, and he always asks me how much of politics is just theater. *Courtesy of the author.*

Sitting with Diana and a passed-out True, watching the returns come in on November 8, 2016. Ours was one of the closest races in the country and therefore one of the last called. Despite outperforming the top of the Democratic ticket by 16 points, we came up just short. *Courtesy of Sam Meers.*

Since Trump took office, I've visited nearly every state, headlined over 160 Democratic events, and been on close to 300 flights. Here I am during a stop in Georgia in 2017. A sense of humor is important if you want to be in politics and stay sane. *Courtesy of the author.*

In February 2017, Abe and I launched Let America Vote with the mission of creating political consequences for voter suppression. Today we have tens of thousands of volunteers nationwide. This was taken in the summer of 2017 at our field office in Manassas, Virginia. *Courtesy of Suzy Smith.*

In 2017, President Trump established a sham voter commission and the Democratic National Committee responded with the Commission on Protecting American Democracy from the Trump Administration and asked me to serve as chair. Here I am in that role, leading a protest of the Trump Commission, which was disbanded a short time later. *Courtesy of Austin Laufersweiler.*

I was invited to keynote the New Hampshire Democratic Party's biggest annual fund-raiser in 2018, and several friends from Missouri came up to join me. Left to right: Karla Thieman, Sly James, me, Jill Schupp, Tishuara Jones, Don Calloway, and Stephen Webber. *Courtesy of Suzy Smith.*

Sore, tired, and having a blast between baseball games at Royals Fantasy Camp in January 2018. *Courtesy of the author.*

As we've gotten a little older, Diana and I have learned to step away from everything occasionally and just appreciate each other. *Courtesy of the author.*

Team Kander. True, me, and Diana. You live your life with your friends and family—not your accomplishments. *Courtesy of Jim Nimmo.*

"You live your life with your friends [and family], not your accomplishments."*

I've tried to justify leaving this part out, but a lesson about life balance won't be truly complete—let alone fully honest—if I don't write about my experience coming home from Afghanistan.

So here goes.

As you read about my comparatively minor difficulties adjusting back to civilian life, keep in mind how much harder it is for the tens of thousands of men and women who saw and did a lot more than me. Again, I was overseas for just a few months, I was never blown up or shot at, and I didn't have to kill anyone, yet it was still the most formative few months of my life, followed by some of the biggest emotional challenges I've faced.

---

* George Brett, in his Hall of Fame induction speech.

I left Afghanistan at night on a C-130 out of Bagram Air Base. There were only a few of us in the cargo bay, so I slept on a pile of duffel bags. We landed in Qatar and I woke up, immediately noticing a muscle spasm in my left eyelid. Every few seconds, the muscle would fire. Merely a minor annoyance, but it lasted about six months and would sometimes spread into the other eye, too.

When I asked a doctor about it, his theory was that I had internalized so much stress during the deployment that it was slowly leaking out in this weird way.

I made use of only a limited set of feelings while I was deployed, because there wasn't a lot of emotional nuance. When I was waiting in line for food, I was bored. When I was laughing and BS-ing with fellow soldiers, I was momentarily happy. When I missed a chance to call home, I was sad and homesick. When preparing to go outside the wire, I felt a sense of focus not unlike a low level of simmering anger. Once outside the wire, if something didn't look right, I felt fear, but the fear was quickly overtaken by a powerful rush of adrenaline.

I'm sure there were other important feelings, like empathy, compassion, and loneliness, but for the most part I found it easier to just keep going to my bag for the same four or five clubs. Of course, I didn't realize any of this at the time, because when everything around you has so suddenly changed, it's pretty difficult to feel yourself changing, too.

When I first came home, it took a little time to remember

how to access all the emotions I experienced with ease before I left. In those first few weeks, Diana and I might be in the middle of a conversation and she'd ask, "What are you so angry about?"

"I don't know," I'd admit.

"Maybe you should go hit the heavy bag," she'd say.

I'd go down to the basement, put on boxing gloves, and whale on a punching bag she'd hung down there during my deployment. It would usually work and make me feel better.

Turns out she'd had her own strategy for all of this while I'd been gone. On our phone calls, she'd act like everything was normal and nothing was bothering her. We got into a couple of arguments over the phone while I was deployed, but neither was significant enough to be memorable. I genuinely thought she was dealing with the whole thing with a level of ease no one ever had before, but once I was home she told me the truth.

As the spouse of a reservist, she didn't know anyone else going through what she was going through, so she didn't have much of a support network. She had read about how dangerous it could be for soldiers in combat zones when they were distracted by problems back home, so she resolved to never let me worry about how things were with "us."

She had gone so far as to try to just accept the reality that I was not coming home. She thought that if she pre-emptively accepted my death, it might not hurt so much if or when she found out about it.

A deployment can sometimes be worse for the person

who stays home than for the person who leaves. Over in Afghanistan, I was challenged every day. It was—if nothing else—exciting and different. I suddenly had all these new friends and coworkers, and while I was sometimes scared for my safety, other times I was simply bored or even asleep.

But for the person who stays home, the only thing that's changed is that the most important human being in that person's life is gone and may never come back. The trash still has to go out, the lawn still has to be mowed, and the chores have to be done, but each task is just a reminder of absence—a shot of sadness with a chaser of concern.

While I averaged an hour or two outside the wire several days a week, Diana was forced to live out there from the moment I left until the moment I came home.

She dealt with this by fighting. Literally. Diana signed up for Krav Maga, a form of mixed martial arts with origins in the Israeli military. She never did it competitively, but she sparred and did the whole routine several days per week. By the time I got home, she was insanely fit and covered in bruises.

So that's why we had a heavy punching bag in the basement.

———

Then there were my bad dreams.

For the first couple of years after coming home, Afghanistan memories replayed in my sleep, only with different, horrific endings. Given the nature of my job over there, I had been worried less about being shot or blown up and more about being kidnapped, and now that I was back in my own bed, it seemed that the Taliban captured me every night.

These bad dreams cost me a lot of sleep, not just because it was hard to fall back to sleep, but also because it made me dread bedtime in the first place, and so I would find excuses to stay up late.

This swell thing called sleep paralysis, in which my mind woke up but my body remained asleep and I couldn't move, accompanied the nightmares. It would last anywhere from two to twenty seconds, but it felt like so much longer. As a bonus, I also had this intense sensation of whatever was threatening me in the dream being in the room and moving toward me, so I'd start to panic and become desperate to sit up and defend myself.

Oftentimes my eyes would open; I could move them and see the room, and I could make low guttural sounds by altering my breathing, but I couldn't move anything else. Other times I would feel like there was something on my chest and I couldn't breathe at all. Diana is a light sleeper, and she came to know the sounds of these episodes, so she'd often wake up, roll over, and shake my body awake. The worst was when I'd make the breathing sounds to alert her and she wouldn't wake up, because that just made it feel like it lasted even longer.

I went and saw a guy about it and he gave me some

helpful tips, like what not to eat before bed. I also declared a personal moratorium on movies and books about war.

A few months later, I took a steep turn off a highway exit a little too tightly just as my tires found some gravel. My car fishtailed and the tires bounced hard off a curb. The car and I were fine because only the tires had made impact, but I pulled off into a parking lot and came to a stop.

My heart was pounding and I'd broken out in a sweat. I looked in the mirror and noticed I was smiling, which wasn't exactly what I'd expected. I felt...fantastic!

I hadn't experienced that level of adrenaline in months, and now I realized my body had missed it. That's why in the first few weeks at home, my pulse shot up every time I got in a car, because for the previous four months in Afghanistan, I'd been in a vehicle only to go outside the wire.

It felt like watching one of those movies where a big, unexpected plot twist is followed by a flashback montage of all the hints you'd missed over the previous two hours.

I ran back through all of it: the punching bag, the eye twitch, the bad dreams, the anger I'd felt watching the news, and I realized it wasn't just me—it was, as someone had once described it to me, "a normal reaction to an abnormal situation."

I researched post-traumatic stress, and it turned out that's probably not what I was dealing with, but I also learned about "battlemind" and the debriefings on it I'd never received from the army.

I had been feeling inadequate and inauthentic about the

issues I was experiencing because, to me, I hadn't "seen anything" really bad over there. But when I read about the concept of battlemind, I realized the impact of the several days a week I'd rolled through the front gates and prepared myself emotionally to, if necessary, take a life.

And now I was just supposed to go back to being a Kansas City lawyer.

Eventually, the eye twitch went away, and as the years have passed, the bad dreams and sleep paralysis have almost entirely taken a hike. When they do come back, it's in a totally different context. Rarely is the setting Afghanistan anymore. Thankfully, the nighttime stuff is far from common these days.

I already had a fairly strong protective instinct, and clearly the training, the deployment, and fatherhood* dialed it up and made the instinct somewhat permanent, but I've learned how to manage it. I can even watch movies or read books about war without a problem—though I prefer not to do either immediately before falling asleep.

My professional success has nothing to do with how much

---

* When I was deployed, I thought very little about what I was putting my poor parents through. Looking back, I remember even calling and saying things such as "I'm going out on a mission, so you won't hear from me for a few days" when I could have fibbed and said, "They're doing maintenance on the phones, so you won't hear from me for a bit." I didn't understand how careless I'd been until six years later when I became a dad. Five minutes after meeting my son, I walked out into the waiting area to retrieve my parents and take them back to see their grandson. The first thing I said to my mom was, "I'm sorry about Afghanistan."

better I feel today, but my family and my friends (including several fellow veterans) have everything to do with it.

The part I still carry with me more than any other is the guilt. When I left Afghanistan, I said good-bye to a few people who were there when I first arrived. And once I came home, I struggled to enjoy little things like a glass of milk or a day off, because I didn't believe I'd earned them. People I knew were still there—and so were people I didn't know.

I can remember being out to dinner, seeing people having a good time with friends and thinking, *Don't these people know what's going on over there? How can everyone act like everything's fine?*

And then sometimes I'd be able to put all that down for an hour or two, long enough to enjoy a night out with Diana or an afternoon catching up with friends, only to feel guilty for having lost perspective. I'd go from *How can everyone act so normal?* to *How the hell can I act like everything's fine now?*

It doesn't hang over me the way it once did, but that guilt—a lingering question of whether I did enough—is always there in the background of my life, pushing me to do what a soldier would do.

Follow your guilt compass.

When I was about fourteen years old, while hanging out at the home of a friend whose family lived paycheck-to-paycheck, my friend's mother told me, "Jason, what I like about you is that you know you've been given a good deal in life and you don't bother to pretend to have had it tough."

That really stuck with me, and I've always tried to catch myself when I've been tempted to let someone believe I've had to navigate a hard-luck road. I've known politicians whose origin stories are genuinely about overcoming adversity from a young age, and I consider that perspective immensely valuable. I also recognize that it's not my perspective.

I grew up comfortably. I'm well aware that—in some respects—even my military service is a reflection of my having grown up privileged enough to make career choices without having to make income a primary factor. The first time I learned what it was like to be on the receiving end of politically driven, bad decisions, I was in the backseat of an unarmored Mitsubishi Pajero in Afghanistan. That's not a hard-luck story—that's a story about living outside the wake of politicians all the way in to my midtwenties.

As I mentioned, I went outside the wire on average about four times a week in Afghanistan, including as part of several convoys.* The simple odds are that on more than one occasion somebody looked at me and weighed whether or not to spring their ambush or trigger an IED or just do nothing at all. For whatever reason, I didn't get blown up

---

* By far the scariest route I ever traveled was Kabul to Jalalabad and back through the Jalalabad Pass. Google it and you'll see why.

or shot at a single time, and that had absolutely nothing to do with skill on my part.

In a combat zone, timing matters, and there is almost nothing you can do to control it. I still feel a tinge of inferiority when I'm around someone who experienced different timing, but logically I know I wouldn't trade places, because who knows if I'd be here today?

My fortunate timing has always added to my sense of guilt, but I've learned to listen to that guilt, and it often serves me well. In fact, guilt led to one of the smallest but most important accomplishments of my time in the secretary of state's office.

Once, while driving home from Jefferson City to Columbia, I saw a man who looked to be about my own age standing by the road, holding a "Will work for food" sign. Sometimes veterans can spot one another the way dogs at stoplights stare at each other from separate cars. We just know military bearing when we see it.

Instinct told me this guy was a vet and that timing hadn't been as kind to him as it had to me, so I pulled off the road, got out of my car, and walked up to him.

"Jason Kander," I said, extending a hand, which he shook firmly while looking me in the eye.

"Justin Coil. Nice meeting you."

"What branch were you in, Justin?"

"Army, sir. You?"

I noticed the rank insignia of a staff sergeant hanging from a chain around his neck.

"Same. What'd you do downrange, Sergeant Coil?"

He smiled at the familiar old feeling of being addressed with respect, and then he opened right up to me. If you've ever witnessed two veterans who've never met being introduced, you've probably noticed it takes no time at all for them to start talking like old friends.

"Iraq. I was in transportation—hit an IED. Came home with TBI and PTSD."*

"Roger. I was a captain, military intelligence, deployed to Afghanistan, but you did a lot more than me."

"A captain, huh? Should I be at attention, sir?" he asked with a smile.

"Nah, now I'm just a long-haired civilian like you." We both laughed a little. Neither of us had grown our hair out much at all.

"So I take it you're self-medicating?" I asked.

"I was. Tried about every drug they got, sir. Had some legal trouble, too."

Over the next few minutes, I learned Justin was homeless, estranged from his wife and child, and currently clean. He wanted to work, but a minor paperwork issue with his service record was holding him back. When you're down and out like he was, the tiniest obstacle can feel like a mountain.

I wasn't able to convince Justin to accept help during that first visit, but I never passed him without getting out of the

---

* Traumatic brain injury and post-traumatic stress disorder.

car and trying again. A few roadside conversations later, he agreed to let my staff help him navigate the system.

Months later, Justin came to my office with good news. Over an hour-long chat, I learned he had an apartment, a job, and a relationship with his family. He was in school part-time and had even been volunteering with a local initiative to build a shelter for homeless veterans.

"Hey, sir, out of curiosity, why'd you stop to help me?" he asked as I walked him out.

"I guess I just saw a veteran my age and thought I should."

"Yeah, but I wasn't easy to help, so why'd you keep coming back?"

"Because what happened to you in Iraq could just as easily have happened to me in Afghanistan, in which case I could've been the one standing out there holding a sign."

"Makes sense," he said with a nod. "If the roles were reversed, I'd probably have kept coming back, too."

"I know," I said.

Stop and celebrate—with or without a gordita.

The first time I ever ate Taco Bell, I was impaired, which is probably why I still think it's the best-tasting thing on earth. A kid at my high school threw a "My parents are out of town" party. I was drinking beer and, for the first time in my young life, I was feeling the effects of alcohol. I was seventeen.

Up until then, Taco Bell food always looked nasty to me and I'd never tried it. But absent my inhibitions, I housed a couple of Santa Fe Beef Gorditas,* and my life was changed. For the rest of high school, I couldn't get enough of Taco Bell.

The habit followed me to college. My freshman year roommates Mel and Andy were both fellow Kansas Citians, and the three of us would take a train and then walk a mile just to have lunch at Taco Bell. We once took a few friends with us who weren't from the Midwest and thus not as appreciative of processed fast food. I was quietly (or so I thought) enjoying my gorditas when everyone stopped eating and just looked at me funny. Mel broke the awkward silence by explaining to them, "Sorry. Jason sometimes moans when he eats Taco Bell."

Anyway, Taco Bell took a toll, and I eventually became a bit soft in the middle. And on the sides. And—judging by the pictures—in the neck, too. Look, I got chubby for a minute in college, OK?

Once 9/11 happened and I started running to get in shape for the army, I realized I had to change the way I ate—or at least I realized I couldn't eat Taco Bell quite so

---

* Taco Bell discontinued the Santa Fe style a few years later. Taco Bell, if you're reading this, please bring it back. You've made a terrible mistake.

often. That's when I established the Taco Bell Rewards System.

Anytime I'd accomplish what I deemed a "physical feat," I'd reward myself with a trip to "The Bell." I don't know how other programs did it, but in the Hoya Battalion (Georgetown's ROTC unit) we took the Army Physical Fitness Test (APFT) once a month. I sometimes cut it a little close, but I never failed one, so during law school, I rang The Bell about once a month.

In intelligence school, we took the APFT three separate times, but I actually ate at Taco Bell four times, because Fort Huachuca, Arizona, is where I, alongside an army buddy, completed what remains to this day my greatest physical feat.

In addition to testing marksmanship, first aid, and knowledge of chemical weapons procedures, the German Armed Forces Proficiency Badge (GAFPB) involves a long swim, a timed thousand-meter sprint, and a sixteen-mile ruck march. The standards have since been significantly relaxed, but I won't give in to the urge to go on a rant about how back in my day it was much harder.

The sixteen-mile ruck march* was the final event and the hardest to pass, and in order to save time, several of us chose to do it in conjunction with the twelve-mile ruck

---

* "Ruck" is a reference to the rucksack, a big green backpack we wear. You may also have heard a "ruck march" referred to as a "road march" or a "forced march."

march we had to pass at the completion of intelligence training. For the twelve-mile ruck, we were required to wear our Kevlar helmets and equipment vests while carrying a rifle and "humping"* a heavy ruck.

The GAFPB ruck march was four miles longer, but the only other requirement was that you carry a comparatively lighter ruck. My buddy Paul and I decided we were tough enough to just combine the two ruck marches, so at the twelve-mile mark, when most of our classmates were celebrating completion, we and a few others dropped weight from our rucks, shed our helmets and our load-bearing vests, took off our boots, bandaged some pretty nasty blisters, changed our socks, and set out to finish the last four miles. We carried our rifles the entire way because even though it wasn't required for the GAFPB, that's the one piece of equipment you're never allowed to set down and come back for later.

The whole thing had to be completed in a certain amount of time, and since we knew back at mile one that we might make a go for it at mile twelve, we'd spent the entire sixteen miles alternating between "humping" and "range walking" (a cooler, army way to say "speed walking").

We also had to carry enough water to last the whole ruck, but I ran out during mile thirteen, and, as I entered

---

* Not what you think. "Humping" is army-speak for the act of running during a ruck march. I always found it funny when the older instructors would tell stories of their "longest" or "best" humps.

the sixteenth and final mile, the leg cramps started. Without slowing down, we managed to take turns drinking from the camelback hose on Paul's shoulder.

The last one hundred meters were some of the toughest steps I've ever taken. My calves felt like clinched fists, and the bandages I'd prepared four miles ago had proven no match for the blisters on my feet.

Paul and I crossed the finish line with just six minutes to spare and hurled ourselves into the bed of a waiting pickup truck. On the drive back to our equipment and our vehicles, we lay on our backs with the wind rushing over us. Smiling and staring up at the stars, we whooped, hollered, and hooah'd to mark the success of "Fire Team Lawyer." Paul and I were two of the three law school graduates in our intelligence school class, and even though we were one short of a fire team, we coined the term on the first day and stuck with it.

When the pickup dropped us off at our own cars, I was so cramped up and dehydrated I could barely move.

"Kander, I hope you're not really going to do your stupid Taco Bell ritual tonight," said Paul.

"What? Of course I'm doing it."

"That's a bad idea, dude."

"Eh, I'll be fine! I earned this!"

"You're gonna regret it," said Paul, but I ignored him.

I got to my room loaded down with my standard haul: two gorditas, one soft taco, and a Diet Pepsi. I drew a hot bath, climbed in, broke into my bounty, and savored the sweet taste of victory.

On my third unsuccessful attempt to get out of the bathtub, I decided Paul had been right. My body needed water and electrolytes, not sugar and saturated fat.

I eventually made it out of that tub (without help)—a physical feat worthy of being added to the GAFPB as an alternate swim test.

Now that I'm out of the army, I don't have quite so many physical feats to accomplish, so I tend to treat myself to Taco Bell about once a year when I achieve something special like reaching a fund-raising goal, finishing a book draft, or…finding myself in an airport with no other food option. It doesn't feel as special without the sense of earning it, but it's still worth it.

Gorditas are just so dang good.

Life is a team sport.

After years of hurrying through life so fast we'd often breeze right past milestone moments, Diana and I now make a habit of pausing briefly to celebrate successes. Sometimes it's small stuff like meeting a personal workout goal (usually her) or landing a client (always her), and sometimes it's been bigger stuff like my winning a court case or her book* getting published in an additional language.

---

* *All In Startup*—it's a business novel about an entrepreneur trying to save his company while simultaneously advancing in the World Series of

Usually we just go out to dinner together (not at Taco Bell—she doesn't share my habit), but it's important to slow down long enough to clink glasses and say, "I'm proud of you."

Perhaps my giving you marriage advice is a bridge too far for this book, but allow me to pass you this one piece of wisdom: once you and your partner find each other, work as a team in everything you do—especially in making the world a better place.

My first date with Diana was my senior prom. We both were seventeen, and by age twenty-two we were married, so we've pretty much grown up together. Nineteen years later, when we're apart and something special happens to me, it doesn't even feel real until the moment I tell her about it.

We both have active careers, but for the past fifteen years or so, we've taken to referring to ourselves as "Team Kander." There's no Jason's career and Diana's career. There's just the two of us trying to boost each other up, root each other on, and do absolutely everything we can to help each other.

Diana wrote her book while on the road with me during the 2012 campaign. In fact, she wrote most of it from the backseat of Abe's Ford Escape. Every time I pick it up and turn to a random page, I'm blown away by it, and I'm as proud of it as I would be had I written it myself.

Poker. Since it was first published in 2014, more than seventy colleges and universities have used it in their business school curricula.

You live your life with your friends and family.

When I was elected secretary of state, she was as happy for me as I was, if not more. We go out of our way to view all the work we do as "ours."

So far, our Team Kander approach is working pretty well. When our son was born and the doctor placed him in Diana's arms, she looked down at him and said, "Welcome to the team, True."

That remains the best moment of my life.

Be willing to fail...publicly.

When strangers saw me in uniform and thanked me for my service, I wasn't sure how to respond. With so many soldiers among my friends, service seemed common to me, and given how many of those friends were doing so much more than I was, I sometimes felt awkward about accepting people's gratitude.

I appreciated the gesture, but I didn't fully understand what moved someone to offer it.

My final drill weekend took place at the Missouri National Guard headquarters in Jefferson City in late 2011. I turned in my gear, signed a form, and that was that.

As I walked across the parking lot to my car, a warrant officer I didn't know got out of his car and headed toward the armory. *This will probably be my last salute*, I thought.

About ten paces before passing me, he offered a "Hooah, sir," as the tip of his index finger met the brim of his soft cap. Taking in the moment, I hesitated a split second longer than usual, and then returned his salute and his "Hooah."

As I drove home, I pondered who I was now. *What am I feeling right now?* I asked myself. Even though I'd been a reservist, I'd long viewed myself as a soldier first, and it was difficult to come to terms with the shift from soldier to veteran. I saw myself as a protector, not as a protectee— but also as part of something bigger than myself. So much of who I was, in my mind, was linked to my affiliation with the army and my connection to a group of people I so admired. To me, leaving the army before doing twenty years and retiring felt a lot like quitting, or at least like failing to finish.

Two and a half hours later, I pulled into our driveway, went inside, kissed Diana, and changed out of my uniform for the last time. I thought of all the times I'd lain down on the couch, groaning from sore muscles and exhaustion, recounting stories from the drill weekend while Diana lovingly unlaced my boots and pulled them off my feet.

She knew I was feeling down and suggested I take her out on a date.

We stopped for gas on the way to dinner, and as I stood between the car and the pump, I noticed a soldier in uniform fueling up about forty feet away. It was a Sunday night, so he had to be a reservist or a guardsman on his way home from drill.

Now that I was on the other side of the protective line, I felt indebted to this person I didn't know. I finally understood why people in airports had felt the urge to thank me all those times.

Today, when I see someone in uniform, I usually strike up a conversation that ends with my saying, "You're still doing it and I'm not, so thank you."

So formative was my army experience that even the act of leaving brought its own lesson for the future: you are more than your title or position—so don't live in fear of losing either.

Drink water and drive on.*

We had the momentum. Our polling indicated we were going to win by a few points, and, from what I'd heard, Senator Blunt's polling had him trailing as well. A twenty-one-month campaign that began with no one giving us a chance had ended with most people convinced we would win.

I started Election Day 2016 in St. Louis, stopped at polling places there and all along I-70, voted in Columbia with Diana and True, and ended at a Kansas City watch party surrounded by my friends and family.

After the polls closed, we got word of exit polling that had us winning handily. Our confidence only grew when the absentee numbers came in from Greene County. The general rule of thumb is that a Democrat needs about 38

---

* Standard army remedy for crushing disappointment.

percent of the Greene County absentees to have a shot statewide. Greene County, home to Springfield and a whole mess of Republican voters, usually came in first and was a reliable bellwether. If you could manage your margin of loss in Greene, you had a chance.

Four years earlier, in 2012, we had actually come in just under 38 percent in Greene County absentees, yet we went on to win. Senator Blunt was from Greene. He won his first election there while Richard Nixon was president. So in the early evening of November 8, 2016, when we learned we had won 44 percent of the absentee vote in Greene County, everything seemed to be going our way.

Abe and the team walked me through the run of show for my victory speech. I met the teleprompter operator, and then I retired to a room by myself to practice. It had really been a spectacular day.

The night, however, kinda sucked.

You know what happened next. The bottom dropped out, Donald Trump appeared headed for a win, and almost all my fellow Democratic Senate candidates lost, too.

A couple of tense hours went by in which our own numbers were still looking strong. Then, when the cities came in, turnout was just short of the boost we needed.

Ours was one of the last major races in the country called for the Republicans. I phoned Senator Blunt and congratulated him.

We gathered the staff backstage so I could address them. I thanked them for all they'd done and implored them not to let this discourage them or chase them out of the fight. "When we made the decision to run, Abe and I vowed to wage a campaign that held nothing back and never let up. A campaign so strong that we would either win or, if not, know definitively it was because we ran in a year when victory couldn't be achieved. I want you to know how proud I am to know we all did exactly what Abe and I vowed to do in the first place and that there's nothing—not one moment—I'd do differently," I said.

The looks on their faces were devastating. Several were in tears, and Diana was consoling a young volunteer she'd only just met. He buried his head in her shoulder and sobbed.

"You've spent the last year or more of your life trying to get me a job," I said. "Now I'll spend the next few months trying to make sure you get whatever job you want next, so get me lists of who you need me to call. That's my campaign for the rest of the year."

I ended abruptly because it was time to walk out and deliver a concession speech we'd never written or even given a second's thought.

I had planned to change into a freshly pressed suit for the victory speech; I didn't feel like changing for a concession speech, so I borrowed a blue tie from Abe and found a mirror. Staring at my reflection and donning the tie, I searched for words I could offer the crowd and the cameras.

What am I feeling right now? I asked myself. The answer was a genuine concern about what these results might do to quash hope among my own generation. *We can't allow millennials to interpret something as horrendous as the election of Donald Trump as a cue to check out for good*, I thought. It was a heavy, dispiriting notion, and I felt genuine fear for America's future.

As I stepped onto the stage, I was determined to make the case for continuing the fight and to put on notice anyone who expected this generation to slink away.

No one had removed the teleprompter displaying the first few words of what would have been my victory speech, but I refused to let that little twist of the knife distract me.

Trying to lend some perspective, I reminded the crowd that America had survived big challenges, including a civil war, and we'd get through this, too. "The thing about elections," I said, "is that we have them pretty often."

After staying long enough to hug anyone who needed a hug, Diana and I turned to Abe and asked him what time he wanted to have breakfast.

At about three in the morning, I woke up and couldn't go back to sleep. I know it's hard to believe, but I wasn't thinking about what the results meant for me; I was thinking about my parents and my brother Jeff and his wife, Sasha, who were on the Obamacare exchange. I woke Diana up to talk about the fact that they were all probably going to lose their health care.

The next morning, at breakfast, Diana was determined not to let me (or Abe) wallow in disappointment.

"Whatever we do, we aren't breaking up this band," she said. We left unsure what was next, but knowing we had no choice but to stay in the fight and to do it together.

I spent most of Wednesday in a fog. A former politician who had lost a couple of elections over the years called to warn me against "underestimating the restorative power of sleep," so I slept as much of that day as I could. I slept in on Thursday morning, too. I knew I should go through the formality of writing a thank-you letter to my supporters, but doing so didn't sound like much fun.

That evening, as I sat unshaven on the couch, Diana reminded me that many others in the country were feeling the way I was, and that some might still be looking to me for leadership.

"You can't do much to make yourself stronger right now," she said, "but you can be strong for them."

Her words reminded me of something we used to say in the army when we were at our most cold or tired: "False motivation is still motivation. HOOOOOAH!"

I thought about the headline of an article in a national publication someone had texted me that morning: "Who is Jason Kander, and why is his concession speech drawing attention?" My message from Tuesday night had hit a nerve, so if I could put aside my own crushing disappointment and focus on motivating others, perhaps I could do something useful.

Drink water and drive on, I thought.

I opened my laptop and—instead of a typical thank-you e-mail—I wrote a more coherent version of what I'd been trying to say in my concession speech less than forty-eight hours earlier.

Thursday, November 10, 2016*

This is the message where I'm supposed to thank you for all you've done for me, tell you how much it meant to me, and then say my goodbyes and wish you luck on your journey. I'm supposed to say something like, "Perhaps our paths will cross again."

But that's not how I roll. Of course, I am thankful to you and I'm forever grateful for this experience. But why wouldn't I be? Let's talk about something important...

If you were a part of this campaign in even the smallest way, you might feel like stepping away from it all to lick your wounds...

Well, you won't get a pass from me. Staying engaged has become more important than ever...

To truly care about this country is to demonstrate that you care about her politics the same when you're winning as when you're losing...

Take some time off...

Ok, was that enough time?

We have work to do. You in?

---

* For an unabridged version, check out JasonKander.com/NoPass.

After sending that e-mail and responding to as many of the thousands of replies as I could, my energy picked up quite a bit, but I remained vulnerable to occasional moments of despair that only Diana got to see. For a couple of weeks, I dreaded going out in public because everyone who recognized me acted as though we'd just bumped into each other at my funeral. "I'm so sorry for you!" they'd say.

A few days after the election, I took True to a dinosaur exhibit at a museum on a weekday. Having declared it one of our "Daddy and True Days," I was in pretty good spirits. A group of fourth graders on a field trip came up to ask if I was "the real Jason Kander." When I said yes, they didn't offer any condolences, they just got really excited, like fourth graders do, and asked a lot of funny questions about politics and being on television. They requested a group picture, and True and I obliged them.

As much fun as that could have been, it left me feeling kind of embarrassed and self-conscious, and I shared as much with Diana at dinner.

"Did any of the kids say they were sorry you lost?" she asked.

"No."

"They were just excited to meet you, right?"

"Yeah."

"Then why do you feel embarrassed about it?"

"I don't know," I said. "I guess I just feel like they see me as a loser right now."

"Out of the six million people who live in this state,

you were the one who went for it," she said. "When people want to meet you, it's because you're one of the very few people in the arena, not because you didn't win."

I just kind of shrugged, but she kept going.

"If you met someone who went to the Olympics but didn't get a medal, would you think of them as a loser?"

"Well, no," I admitted.

"Those kids don't see someone who didn't get gold. They see an Olympian. That's what everyone sees but you."

As always, Diana set my perspective where it needed to be, and from then on, I was reenergized and back in the fight.

My postelection experience isn't limited in its relevance to those thinking of running for office or working on campaigns. In the age of social media, all failure feels public. If you lose your job, your friends are all going to know about it when you update your LinkedIn profile, and if your spouse leaves you and updates his or her "relationship status" on Facebook, the same friends will know about that, too.

Recall what then Missouri attorney general Chris Koster told me as I stared at that screen and decided whether to jump headfirst into a race for secretary of state: "If you're willing to fail, you're very dangerous to the status quo."

Or, as a pitching coach once said to me after I gave up five runs in one inning: "Kander, go home, drink a bunch of Ex-Lax, get all that shit out of your system, and I'll see you at practice tomorrow."

Make your argument.

When I ran for secretary of state in 2012, everyone in Missouri politics knew the biggest issue in the race would be photo identification. For years, Missouri Republicans had been trying to pass a law requiring voters to present their driver's licenses at the polls in order to cast their ballots.

Given that well over 70 percent of Missourians disagreed with my opposition to photo ID requirements, some of my advisers asked me to reconsider my position.

I said no, because laws requiring voters to present photo identification at the polls don't prevent fraud; they prevent voting.

As an American, you are statistically more likely to be struck by lightning than you are to commit voter impersonation fraud, and in the history of Missouri, there has never been a report of it happening even once. However, there are more than two hundred thousand legally registered Missouri voters who don't have a driver's license, and a disproportionate number of them are in demographic groups that rarely vote Republican, which gets at the real reason Republicans want photo ID laws in the first place: to stop people who vote against them from being allowed to vote.

My opponent's main television ad featured him talking about photo ID while showing off his own driver's license. When I refused to change my position, advisers suggested I try to ignore the issue, but I said no to that, too, because you lose 100 percent of the arguments you don't make.*

To this day, I'm the only candidate for secretary of state in a competitive general election anywhere in the country to run a statewide ad *highlighting* my opposition to photo ID. Arguing it would have made it nearly impossible for me to vote from Afghanistan in 2006, I explained how much it meant to me to participate in the very democracy I was over there to protect, and I promised to make sure no eligible voter ever had that right taken away.

On Election Day, I stood outside polling places shaking hands with voters. As they headed in to vote, a lot of people—unsurprisingly—said to me, "You're wrong about photo ID," but quite a few also lingered long enough to say, "but you told me the truth and I respect your point of view, so you're gonna get my vote today."

That evening, as President Obama lost Missouri by almost ten points, I won, because I'd made my argument.

---

* My apologies to Wayne Gretzky.

Show your math.

When I meet people who take naturally to math, science, or a musical instrument, I feel like I'm meeting a superhero, because all three of those seem like superpowers to me.

Being a poor math student, I came to understand that it would be counted against me on a test if I wrote down an answer the teacher didn't agree with.* But I quickly came to learn that if I showed my math and made it easy to follow the misadventure I traveled on the way to my answer, the teacher would sometimes put a little half-point mark along the side of the path I'd followed.

In politics, not everyone is going to agree with your position, but if you show your math—if you take voters on the personal journey you traveled to reach your opinion—they're more likely to forgive you for coming up with a different answer than they did. But in order to do that, you have to look inside yourself and ask, "Why do I believe what I believe? What is it that's happened in my life that helped me see things the way I do?"

Politics is far more introspective than we give it credit for, because it begins with self-examination and ends with self-explanation. Whether it was the anti–photo ID ad in my secretary of state race or the pro–gun control ad in my Senate race, I looked inside myself, figured out how I reached my opinion, and then shared what I'd learned with voters.

---

* Aka the "wrong" answer.

Most people don't think about politics as often as politicians do.

I recently had a conversation with a young man who went door-to-door for the Democratic Party in Missouri in 2016.

"I met so many Republicans who considered 'Democrat' to be a dirty word," he said, "but then they'd casually tell me they liked you and were going to vote for you. How is that possible?"

"What do you mean?" I asked.

"How is it possible that they hated all Democrats but still voted for the progressive guy who had an F rating from the NRA and was endorsed by Planned Parenthood?"

"They just liked me, I guess," I said.

"But why?" he asked. "What issue position of yours allowed them to justify voting for a progressive Democrat?"

"They didn't have to justify it," I said, "because they're not politicians; they're voters."

I wrote a book about politics, so politics is obviously something to which I've given a fair amount of thought. You're reading the book I wrote about politics, so it's something you've thought a lot about, too. For me, politics is a vocation. Maybe the same is true for you. If not, it is, at a minimum, more than a hobby in your life.

That's not true for most people.

Most voters—even consistent, passionate ones—spend less time thinking about elections than they do about sports or popular culture. This isn't always a bad thing, by the way. We live in a Democratic republic. The whole concept revolves around electing people to make big decisions for us so that we don't have to, and so we can focus on our jobs, our families, and our interests.

Most voters aren't *in politics*, meaning they don't talk about it much with their friends or their coworkers, and therefore they almost never have to justify their political decisions. When most people talk about politics, it's more akin to the way my friends and I talk about baseball.

I'm a Royals fan who lived through the decades when the Royals were horribly bad and operated like a minor-league affiliate of the obscenely good Yankees. This—combined with my knowledge of the Royals-Yankees rivalry of the '70s—made me an avowed Yankee hater. My friends in Kansas City share this view, and yet when I say to them, "Man, Aaron Judge* was an obvious rookie of the year choice, right?," no one calls me out as a "Yankee Hater in Name Only." Instead, they—Yankee haters all—shrug their shoulders and say, "Yeah, can't help but like that kid. Hate those Yankees, though."

None of us are running for high baseball office, and therefore no one demands a consistent line of ideological baseball purity from us. And that's pretty much how it works for voters. Their thought processes might begin something like, "Man, I hate the Democrats—they're

---

* A gargantuan, annoyingly likable, pin-striped person who can hit a baseball very far.

awful people" and still end with, "I like Kander, though, 'cause he seems like an OK guy, so I'm gonna vote for him, but good lord, the Democrats are the worst!"

And none of their friends get upset with them or challenge them about it, because even if they disagree and they don't like me, they're not going to get into a fight about it with their friend. In fact, they might consider voting for me themselves based on their friend's endorsement.

Voters are not going line for line down a scorecard of policy positions trying to see how many places their views match mine, so taking positions I don't believe in won't score me points with people who are just trying to figure out if they like me or not. This isn't a multiple-choice test—it's a job interview.

Again, there is no code to crack; there's just making your argument, because if you do, you might actually convince someone.

Make your argument with courage and make it to everyone.

As secretary of state, I actually expanded voting access while simultaneously fending off the GOP's voter suppression efforts. The Republican supermajority wanted desperately to pass the photo ID requirement, but for most of those years, we stopped them.

During my last full year in office, the Republicans

successfully overrode the governor's veto by striking a deal with Democratic state legislators. Democrats in the state senate, in exchange for several legislative provisions meant to lessen the number of Missourians disenfranchised by the new photo ID law, agreed to end their filibuster.

Basically, the Republicans said, "OK, we'll take most of the teeth out of this thing if we can just say we finally passed a photo ID law."

Passed in 2016, the law was due to take effect in June of 2017. By December 2016, I was beginning to hear rumblings from the legislature. Now that they had a Republican governor and didn't have to worry about gaining enough votes to override a veto, Republican members were talking openly about the need to "finish the job" by going back on their word to Democrats and passing an extreme Wisconsin-style photo ID law.*

A pro–photo ID Republican had won the race to succeed me as secretary of state, so when it came to voting rights, the foxes were surrounding the henhouse.

I had one final chance to make my argument, though.

Every two years, at the beginning of a new Missouri General Assembly, the secretary of state presides over the

---

* In 2016, Wisconsin had the lowest voter turnout in twenty years. Election officials there say the turnout was most depressed in the low-income communities expected to encounter the largest difficulty obtaining a photo ID. One study concluded that at least 16,800 voters *in just two counties* were kept away from the polls by the law. President Trump won the entire state by just 22,748 votes.

opening session of the House of Representatives as it swears in new members and elects a Speaker of the House. It's meant to be purely ceremonial because the majority party has already chosen a Speaker, so the secretary of state, by tradition, delivers a short kumbaya-style speech thanking all the elected officials for serving, swearing them in while their family members watch from the galleries, and then holding a show vote for Speaker.

The thing is, while it's only a formality, the secretary of state does technically have the gavel and the discretion of when to call for the vote, so I had a captive audience.

After swearing in the new members, I began my speech in the tone they'd expect, congratulating everyone on all their work and inviting them to applaud their families as a show of gratitude.

"Now, I know I'm not who you came to hear today," I said, "and most of you are not going to like what I have to say, but I am your secretary of state for a little bit longer."

I launched into a nine-minute speech that St. Louis state representative (and rap artist) Bruce Franks would later call "a battle rap."

I called out the Republicans on their plans to go back on their word and curtail voting rights. I used a few notes but didn't read from a teleprompter, which allowed me to make eye contact with each and every legislator.

I promised I'd be paying attention in my role as a private citizen, and that if they chose to go back on their word, I would find a way to hold them accountable.

When I finished, the Democrats applauded loudly, as did some in the galleries. The Republicans fumed silently, many of them mean-mugging me.* There was noticeable anger hanging in the air as I went about the remainder of my duties in presiding over the process.

When my part was complete and I'd handed over the gavel, I descended the dais and walked with members of my staff out the door and downstairs to the parking lot. I drove straight to my house in Columbia, packed the last of our bags, and left for Kansas City, where True and Diana were waiting for me so we could start the rest of our lives.

Traditionally, a secretary of state doesn't give such a speech in that chamber, but as I mentioned several rules ago, some political traditions are pretty dumb. If hewing to a conventional path and "staying in your lane" means allowing someone to be hurt, you have an obligation to swerve out of your lane and make your argument to everybody.

Despite a supermajority in both chambers, a Republican in the governor's mansion, and a Republican flying my old desk in the secretary of state's building, the legislature still hasn't even gone so far as to debate a new photo ID bill.

There are a lot of people to thank for forcing them to scrap their plans to go back on their word, but I strongly believe calling them out publicly—uncomfortable as it may have been—made a difference.

---

* A few—secretly, of course—called me afterward to thank me for speaking out.

If you want to change a politician's behavior, tattle on them to voters.

Around that same time, I accepted an invitation from a progressive group in Iowa to give a talk about how I'd outperformed the top of the ticket by so much. Abe joined me for the trip. Throughout the night, activists in Iowa kept asking our advice on how to wage a political (rather than just a legal) fight against voter suppression because Republicans had recently taken over the Iowa legislature and proposed a photo ID law. Abe and I were some of the only people in the country who'd ever actually done it, they said.

During the drive back to Kansas City, we talked about the coming Republican assault on voting rights. Then president-elect Trump had just said that three to five million illegal voters voted in the election, and most people chalked it up as just another lie by a deeply insecure human being eager to justify his margin of defeat in the popular vote.

While that's accurate, Abe and I saw the beginning of a voter suppression strategy we had become very familiar with in my role as chief election official of a state with a GOP supermajority in its legislature.

The GOP Voter Suppression Playbook has three steps:

1. Undermine faith in American democracy.
2. Create obstacles to voting.
3. Create obstacles to the obstacles.

President Trump won the election via an inside straight in the Electoral College, and he and his pals are smart enough to know that their best chance to duplicate that strategy is to get every state to adopt antivoting laws like Wisconsin's.

This isn't new. Modern voter suppression has been a key part of the Republican political strategy for almost two decades. They pretend it's a policy difference like taxes or health care, but that's just not true. It's a political strategy no different than when they decide which houses to send mailers to or during which shows to run television ads.

But it's not just photo ID either, because Republicans have a lot of different strategies to suppress the vote: draconian voter roll purges of "foreign-sounding" surnames, "consolidating" urban polling places, closing early voting locations, cutting early voting hours, refusing to restore voting rights to the formerly incarcerated, changing residency requirements to intimidate college students, spreading false information about voting procedures, and even putting law enforcement officers at the polls while spreading social media rumors that they'll be there to check for outstanding warrants.*

For years, voting rights advocates fought back via legal challenges almost exclusively, and that was the appropriate way to do it, because most judges were looking out for

---

* This list of tactics sounds even scarier in the original Russian. (Hey-oh!)

voters in these cases and because for eight years we had a Department of Justice on the job.

But when President Trump named Jeff Sessions his attorney general, that meant the Department of Justice was about to switch sides. Combined with the president filling the courts with his appointees, we were going to have to recognize that while the legal fight would remain crucial, it couldn't be our only way to stand up for voters.

During that drive from Des Moines to Kansas City, Abe and I decided to expand the national voting rights argument beyond the court of law and into the court of public opinion.

We started Let America Vote with the mission of creating political consequences for politicians who push voter suppression. You've heard of Big Oil, Big Tobacco, and Big Pharma; Abe and I decided it was time somebody created Big Voter. Basically, if you're an elected official making it harder to vote, Let America Vote makes it harder for you to get reelected, and—a year and half later—we've had a lot of success in that regard.*

In 2017, our volunteers knocked on hundreds of thousands of doors and, in November, helped remove several vote-suppressing Republicans from office, replacing them with Democrats who are dedicated voting rights advocates. Today, Let America Vote has dozens of staffers and tens of thousands of volunteers spread across several states.

---

* Learn more at LetAmericaVote.org.

When President Trump created the "White House Commission on Election Integrity"* and placed Vice President Pence and my old pal Kris Kobach in charge of it, all of us in the voting rights world knew it was a dangerous stride toward step one of the Voter Suppression Playbook (undermine faith in American democracy).

The commission promised to issue a voter fraud "report" justifying the president's enormous lie about illegal voters and paving the way for changes to state law from coast to coast. On the commission's behalf, Kobach sent every secretary of state a request for the personal information of every registered voter in the country.

In response, the Democratic National Committee created the Commission on Protecting American Democracy from the Trump Administration and asked me to serve as chairman. Between our countercommission and Let America Vote, we literally showed up in numbers and made our argument every time the White House panel reared its lying head.

Groups such as the ACLU brought legal challenges, while Let America Vote volunteers all over the country urged election administrators not to cooperate with Kobach's requests. The work paid off, because after just two commission meetings, President Trump flew the white flag and dissolved the commission by executive order.

So guess what I did?

---

* Better name: "The Voter Suppression Committee to Reelect the President."

I ate some Taco Bell and got right back to work, because the president isn't about to give up his un-American antivoting efforts just because we killed his commission.

I chose this fight because the Republican Party decided to make this the fight to end all fights. Back when I deployed, I was willing to put my life on the line for the rights and freedoms our nation has to offer, so I'll be damned if I'm going to sit by and do nothing while President Trump works to take those rights and freedoms away right here at home.

The least I can do is have the everyday courage to make my argument.

Part of being a progressive is the belief that progressive policies are better for everyone.

Not some people. Not even most people. Everyone.

I believe that a progressive agenda can enhance the life of every single American. Rich or poor. Black or white. Gay or straight. Man or woman. City or country. Everyone.

That seems obvious I suppose, but if it is, why have we been skipping certain voters in making our argument? We should never again write off a single American voter.*

Just about every voter I've ever met wants their family to

---

* Except neo-Nazis and the KKK. I rather like knowing they're voting for someone else.

be happy, healthy, safe, and nearby. That's it. That's what politics is about in this country. We all want our kids' lives to be an upgrade over our own without them having to move away from us to get a quality job.

Whether it's treating health care as a right, raising wages, demonstrating that black lives matter by ending racial bias in the criminal justice system, fighting climate change, making college affordable, reducing gun violence, or standing up for DACA kids, my political views all come back to wanting every American hometown to be a safe, welcoming place full of opportunity.

I'm not saying no one should leave his or her hometown, or even that everybody should go back home. You might choose to move away permanently, but I want it to be your choice, not something you had to do in order to find success.

While my great-great-grandfather was the first Kansas City Kander, Diana came to Kansas City as an eight-year-old refugee of religious persecution from the Soviet Union. We have good jobs and medical care when we need it. We live on a safe street just a twenty-minute drive from True's grandparents, aunts, uncles, and cousins. To me, that's the American dream, and I want everyone in every zip code to achieve it.

That's an argument worth making.

"Something's happening here"* (in America).

"You must be so frustrated by the news these days."

People say that to me all the time, but the truth is, I'm not. I would obviously prefer a different president, a different majority in both houses of Congress, and several other differences in who is and is not in power throughout the country, but I'm not frustrated.

I'm too busy to be frustrated. Between Let America Vote, my *Majority 54* podcast, this book, television appearances, campaigning for candidates, and the grassroots organizing and surrogate work I do around the country, I wake up nearly every day with an opportunity to fight for the cause of progress.

---

* I like that old Buffalo Springfield song, "For What It's Worth," the one that goes, "Stop, hey, what's that sound, everybody look what's goin' down..."

As the old saying goes, "It's very difficult to feel down and useful at the same time."

Loads of progressive Americans sit at desks all day absorbing frustrating news alerts, but the ones who channel that into outlets of activism after work or on the weekends or both are the least likely to be depressed about the direction of the country.

These are "grab an oar" times. If you and your friends are sitting around pondering questions such as, "Will Trump stay in office the entire four years?" then every morning when you wake up and he's still president, you probably have to relive November 9, 2016, all over again.

And that's not helping you or the country.

Patriotism is not about making everyone stand and salute the flag. Patriotism is about making this a country where everyone wants to.

Since President Trump took office, I've visited nearly every state campaigning for Democrats and promoting voting rights. In the spring of 2017, I made one of several visits to Tennessee. A woman named Dawn picked me up at the airport and spent the day driving me from one event to the next. Everywhere we went, walking in with Dawn was like walking into Cheers with Norm, because the room would erupt with, "Dawn!"

Dawn was obviously a longtime, ace number one volunteer of the Tennessee Democratic Party. That evening, as Dawn dropped me off at the airport so I could fly home to Kansas City, I asked her how many years she'd been volunteering with the Tennessee Dems.

"Years? Honey, I got involved on January 20, 2017. Before that, the most I ever did was vote."

I've lost count of how many hundreds of people I've met who—like Dawn—have become nearly full-time activists since President Trump took office.

There's a level of activism in the country right now unlike anything I've seen in my lifetime, and it's not some politician on TV bringing people into the movement. Instead, it's retirees calling their neighbors and saying, "Hey, I know our congressional district is super red, but I'm going to this town hall to demand answers about health care; do you want to come, too?"

It's students organizing Let America Vote chapters and phone banks on their college campuses and moms in red "Moms Demand Action for Gun Sense in America" T-shirts flooding state capitols from coast to coast alongside sixteen- and seventeen-year-old leaders of the #NeverAgain movement.

At a local Indivisible meeting in Iowa City, I met a family of three. The mom was working two jobs, the dad was a union ironworker, and the daughter, Aubrey, was a senior in high school. When I asked who brought whom to the meeting, Aubrey said, "I think we all brought each other." Then she asked my advice on how to run a voter registration drive at her school.

The most effective movements in American history have not started in Washington and gone to the rest of the country; they've started everywhere else and gone to Washington. That's what's happening right now. President Trump may have won the 2016 election, but he didn't win the argument about who we are or where we're going as a nation.

Republicans have the power, but we have the momentum.

Persons in country are much closer than they appear.

Dawn and Aubrey's door knocking, phone calling, and marching aren't just about beating the guys in the Republican jerseys. Americans are taking to the streets not just because they want to win an election or because they want to see the party of Trump lose one; they're taking to the streets because they want to unite their country again. The "resistance" is not the opposite of Trumpism—it's the patriotic, inclusive alternative to division and exclusion.

That may read like a pie-in-the-sky portrayal of the state of American politics and culture, and perhaps you're thinking, "OK, Jason, that sounds nice, but it looks to me like we're coming apart at the seams."

I'll concede it feels that way if you base your assessment

solely on Fox News and social media—both of which tend to accentuate our differences and ignore our common values.

But take it from a guy who's logged hundreds of thousands of frequent-flier miles in the last couple of years: our differences just aren't as numerous as advertised.

I learned this over a decade ago.

Before I deployed, an instructor in intelligence school pulled me aside and—one Jewish soldier to another—told me not to tell any of my translators that I was Jewish, because they wouldn't want to work with me if they found out. I didn't know any better, so I took his advice.

When I got to Afghanistan, I was paired up with a guy named Salam as my primary translator. Salam, by pure coincidence, had family in Kansas City and, like me, considered Kansas City his hometown. We spent a lot of time together, including in some dangerous places and with some shady people. I had never had a Muslim friend I was as close to as Salam, so I asked him a lot of questions about Islam and he always answered, but he never asked about my religion and I never told him.

With a few days left before I was set to return to the United States, I decided to tell Salam I was Jewish. We were at his safe house snacking on leftovers and I made sort of a big production of it.

Salam looked at me funny and asked, "Jason, did you think I didn't know that?"

"Well, yeah," I said. "I mean, I never told you."

"Jason, back home in Kansas City, my sister cuts your grandmother's hair."

We had a good laugh, then the smile left Salam's face and— a little hurt—he asked me if I thought he would care. I was embarrassed, but I told him the advice I had gotten in intelligence school. Then Salam said something I'll never forget.

"Jason, over here we are just a couple of Americans the bad guys would very much like to kill."

Believe.

If the reason you're involved in politics is you, you're doing it wrong.

Every once in a while, someone foolishly implies that I joined the military to set myself up for a political career. No one who's actually served ever makes that suggestion, because anyone who's ever been on a sixteen-mile ruck march or spent a sleep-deprived week in the woods knows that no amount of personal ambition is enough to carry you through. For the toughest of challenges, belief is the only fuel that works, and a belief in your country or the people around you can be enough to power you through the hard times.

To do anything difficult—and particularly to do it well— you have to believe in it.

If you're serious about public service, you have to learn how to be impatient and patient at the same time: impatient enough to stay aggressive in advancing the greatest changes you seek, yet patient enough never to quit on them, no matter how slow progress may come.

Steel yourself to this fact: the grandest change you seek—the dream you're pursuing for the country—may not come to fruition during your lifetime. Now accept the fact that you still have to try, because—as President Obama taught us—progress is a baton we pass to one another, not a finish line we cross. Often, in fact, there is no finish line—there is only making tomorrow better than today.

With all the strategy and gamesmanship and general BS that you have to fly through in politics, don't forget to believe. Politics will try to grind away your inner chinstrap, but don't let it. As Andy told Red in *The Shawshank Redemption*,* "Hope is a good thing, maybe the best of things."

As you go about your ambitious life and career, don't forget to believe in something greater than yourself. Find someone who inspires you, and once you do, it's OK to put some belief into that person, too.

Our country needs people who will get in the Pajero.

For many years, we Americans have had the luxury of staying inside the wire politically. Not just cautious politicians,

---

* The *Citizen Kane* of…eh, I've dragged that joke out far enough. Also, one of these days I should actually see *Citizen Kane*. I hear it's quite something.

but average Americans, too. America's almost unchallenged economic and military supremacy contributed to our unrivaled status as the world's leader, and it felt like a permanent condition. It was a nice, cushy comfort zone we took for granted.

Sure, you disagreed with the other side, but you didn't worry about the future of our country the way you do now, so you didn't feel the compulsion to make it awkward at work by bringing up politics. When your cousin said something nutty on Facebook, you didn't e-mail him about it. Well, those days are in the past.

The world is a safer place for everyone, especially Americans, when we lead it, because we've nearly always been a force for good. We've been about democracy and actual debate. We've been about human rights. Not always, but almost always, we've been good people trying to do the right thing. Right now, every inch of progress we've gained— every stride we hope to make in the future—is in doubt.

So if you're worried about the direction of your country but usually keep your politics to yourself, it's time to change that.

You can talk to family, coworkers, neighbors—heck, you can even talk to the person in line behind you at the grocery store—but it's time we all start talking. This gets done one American to another, one at a time.

Don't worry, you don't have to preach. Ask questions and have a conversation, but get people talking. The First Amendment combined with modern technology means we all have a platform, and I wrote this book because I want you to use yours.

Tweets are not enough. If you're serious about being part of the solution, you can knock on doors, make phone calls, march, call your member of Congress, or organize your friends to do the same. If no organization exists in your community to receive and harness enthusiasm from people like you...congratulations, it does now, and you're the founder.

You can run for office yourself. And don't tell me, "I'm just too honest to run for office," because what you really mean is, "That seems scary." Look around. Honesty is the medicine we need right now.

I still think all the time about the face of that scared kid in Afghanistan as he considered whether or not to get into an unarmored Mitsubishi Pajero. He ultimately did, because he knew climbing into that seat behind me— doing his job—was more important than it was scary. Here at home, I'm looking for people who, like him, choose to do what's right even when it's hard.

Across the generations, we *all* are going to have to experience life outside the political wire, so we'd better start building capacity by developing those habits and muscles.

Americans have been defending this country at home and abroad for generations, but none of them have ever done it from within their comfort zones.

So drink some water, take a deep breath, and mount up. You can ride with me.

Acknowledgments*

I want to begin by thanking my parents: Janet and Steve Kander. Before anyone ever uttered the phrase "Check your privilege," my mom and dad were raising me to understand that with great privilege and opportunity comes equal if not greater responsibility for making the world a better place for people we might never actually meet. Mom and Dad are two of the most remarkable humans I've ever known, and I sometimes can't believe my luck in having them for parents. They gave us everything, never allowed us to pretend we'd had it rough, and taught us about the opportunity we'd been granted to help others.

Diana helped me find my way through this book—just as she helps me find my way through every day of my life.

---

* When I finish a book, I read the acknowledgments section because I want to hear more from the author. Hopefully that's how you feel right now, so let's get in touch. Take a picture of where you were when you finished *Outside the Wire*, and share it on social media. Tag some friends you think would enjoy this book, and tag me so I can thank you for reading it. If you want to hear more from me, find me on Twitter, Facebook, Instagram, and Snapchat, and check out my vlog on YouTube.

I lost count of how many times she let me wake her up in the middle of the night as I read a passage aloud and asked, "What do you think?" This is my first book, and I was writing it while Diana was writing her second book, but she helped me immensely from the initial outline to the presale campaign.

Honestly, I live to show off for her, and it's entirely possible I wrote an entire book just to impress her.

My agent, Tina Bennett of William Morris Endeavor, helped me turn something I wanted to say into something that sounded like a book proposal. She has been an incredible advocate from our very first meeting.

When we began talking to publishers, I knew I didn't want to write either a traditional memoir or a policy manifesto. Several well-meaning publishers proposed ideas along those lines, and while I certainly appreciate their interest, I knew TWELVE was for me when Sean Desmond said he liked my vision for *Outside the Wire* and was ready to run with it.

I wrote most of *Outside the Wire* at thirty thousand feet, and Sean was supportive (and patient) from start to finish.

I also want to thank the rest of the TWELVE team. I'm a rookie author, and Sean's assistant, Rachel Kambury, really helped me understand the publishing process. Jarrod Taylor did a great job with the cover, and Paul Samuelson, Brian McLendon, and Rachel Molland crushed it when it came to promoting this baby. My high school debate coach, Melissa Reynolds, won't have to send me a red-penned copy of *Outside the Wire* (she once did that with one of my fund-raising letters), and that's due entirely to the masterful copyediting of Deborah Wiseman.

Several friends did me the favor of reading a draft and making suggestions, and every one of them helped make this a better book.

Finally, I want to thank Mr. True Steven Kander—who will celebrate his fifth birthday a month after this book hits shelves—for helping me pick out the photos. All True asked in return was that I let him write the book's final word:

Poop.

About the Author

In President Obama's final oval office interview, he was asked whom he thought was the future of the Democratic Party, and the first name he mentioned was Jason Kander's.

A former captain in the United States Army who joined after 9/11, Jason volunteered to serve in Afghanistan as a military intelligence officer, where his commanding officers called him an "outstanding leader" who "volunteered for dangerous duty" and the Afghan intelligence watch commander said his "hard work directly resulted in arresting enemies and saving lives." After his deployment, Jason took an assignment as a leadership instructor for Officer Candidate School, where he trained hundreds of soldiers to lead troops into combat and was one of ten finalists for the reserve officer association's Junior Officer of the Year Award.

After returning home to Kansas City, he was elected to the first of two terms in the Missouri House of Representatives. In 2012, Jason won his race for Missouri secretary of state, making him the first millennial in the country ever elected to a statewide office.

In 2016, he challenged Missouri's incumbent Republican senator in what became—at $75 million—the most expensive race in state history. He lost by one of the closest margins in the country, overperforming the presidential ticket by nearly 16 points and receiving over 220,000 crossover votes, more than any other competitive Senate race in the country that year.

In February 2017, Jason founded Let America Vote, a national voting rights advocacy organization dedicated to creating political consequences for politicians who make it harder to cast a ballot. More than 100,000 grassroots donations and over 70,000 volunteers across the country power Let America Vote.

In addition to his work with Let America Vote, Jason was appointed to chair the DNC's Commission on Protecting American Democracy from the Trump Administration.

After spending a year as a CNN contributor, he now makes regular television appearances on several networks. His Crooked Media–backed podcast, *Majority 54*, debuted at #1 on the podcast charts in 2017.

A graduate of American University and Georgetown Law School, Jason is married to his high school sweetheart, Diana, and they live in Kansas City with their four-year-old son, True.

JUL 3 1 2018